CHAMPION!

EVERYTHING YOU NEED TO BE YOUR GREATEST YOU

CHAMPION!

Dr. Michal Solomonovich & Alon Ulman

First published in the UK and USA in 2023 by Watkins, an imprint of Watkins Media Limited, Unit 11, Shepperton House, 83–93 Shepperton Road, London N1 3DF

enquiries@watkinspublishing.com

Design and typography copyright © Watkins Media Limited 2023

Text and Artwork copyright copyright © Watkins Media Limited 2023

Commissioning Editor: Lucy Carroll

Managing Editor: Daniel Culver

Head of Design: Karen Smith

Designer: Sarah O'Flaherty

Production: Uzma Taj

A CIP record for this book is available from the British Library

ISBN: 978-1-78678-750-7 (Paperback)
ISBN: 978-1-78678-762-0 (eBook)

10 9 8 7 6 5 4 3 2 1

Printed in China

www.watkinspublishing.com

CHAMPION!

EVERYTHING YOU NEED TO
BE YOUR GREATEST YOU

DR. MICHAL SOLOMONOVICH
& ALON ULMAN

WATKINS

Dedicated to all our readers.
We hope we can give you some of
the things in these pages that we
didn't have when we were young.

Table of Contents

Introduction

HELLO, CHAMPION,

Who doesn't want to live a happy, successful and fulfilling life? The question is, how can we do that? Creating your dream life can feel impossible, but you've already taken the first big step: you're holding this book in your hands and you've started reading it! You've decided to invest time and effort in yourself (and we know you have plenty of other things to do, but here you are!) and that says a lot about you. Congratulations, you're the type of person who tries to be the best they can possibly be. You are already a champion! We're here to teach you how to be successful in all aspects of life: school, your personal life, sports and hobbies—and anywhere else you want to succeed.

We've been exactly where you are now and remember asking ourselves questions like "What do I really want to do when I grow up?", "How can I be successful and happy?", "How do I juggle school, sports and a social life?", "How do I cope with failure?". Believe it or not, we know what we're talking about. Alon is an entrepreneur, writer and lecturer, and has helped about 400 large organizations and thousands of people reach their goals and targets. Michal has a PhD in education, is an NLP Master (helping people change their thoughts and behavior to achieve positive results), a personal coach with expertise in kids and teens coaching and in ADHD coaching, and lectures in front of students, principals, teachers and parents. Alon has successfully taught the methods in this book to adults for years. Michal applied these to her own family and saw how well her kids were doing, she initiated the adaptation of the method to children and teens for the purpose of helping more young people achieve their goals together. So, that's exactly what we're here to do, and make those questions we mentioned earlier a little easier to answer.

We really hope this book will save you from some of the hardships we've had to face. We've divided it into ten clear codes for success you can apply to your life right now. Think for a moment about the word **'code'**—a collection of words or numbers. Much like a secret code, Morse code, or a special language that we will learn how to use this book is a code that will navigate you toward success. We will lead you, hand in hand, in practical and clear steps, toward being your greatest you. We want to help you achieve your goals with an intensity and speed you have never seen before! You will be amazed at how quickly you can make a difference. Our goal is to give you what we didn't have at your age—the knowledge and tools, as well as the method, mentoring and supportive environment to succeed in life. So, with that said, we invite you on the most interesting journey in the world—and that is your own journey of self-discovery!

LOVE,
MICHAL AND ALON

Code 1

Trust the Process

"TEN INCHES of learning about YOURSELF are WORTH more than TEN MILES of THEORY"

(Alon Ulman)

IN THIS CHAPTER, WE'LL EXPAND ON WHAT WE TALKED ABOUT IN THE INTRODUCTION. WE'LL ALSO SHOW YOU HOW TO USE THIS BOOK AND GET THE MOST OUT OF IT, SO YOU CAN ACHIEVE YOUR GOALS.

SUCCESS IS NOT A FLUKE

We don't know each other yet, but we'll get to know each other as you read along. You may not read many books these days. Maybe you're just too busy, or you don't think they are very helpful for you in your everyday life. However, this book is different, we promise you!

Do you ever feel like everyone else is living their best life but you're not quite sure how to? That's where this book comes in. In life, there are clear codes for success that we can teach you, so, before you know it, you'll be living your best life too. We call that **practical success**.

Sounds mind blowing, right?! What does that even mean?

Success

Reaching a set goal or target, getting a good result, or meeting the required conditions. Think about the things you have accomplished in life: for example, getting a good grade, making a sports team, making new friends and so on.

Practical

A practical person actually engages in life and doesn't just theorize or think about doing things.

Practical SUCCESS

This field has existed in the adult world for years, but for young people it's a new concept. We're going to show you **how to make your dreams come true** by teaching you practical things that will actually help you achieve in every aspect of your life: **at school, in your social life, at home** and anywhere else you want to succeed.

DREAMS COME TRUE

Another STEP FORWARD

The idea behind the codes is for you to live a happy life in which you fulfill your goals, not only one time, but all the time, **as a way of life**. Have you ever noticed that some people seem to succeed all the time and make it look easy? This doesn't actually mean there's no effort behind their achievement. It means they have learned how to apply themselves every time. We want you to look back and see how far you have come—and it will seem as if it wasn't as hard as you thought it was going to be. Other people might even think you made that look easy and effortless. However, practically speaking, of course, a lot of work has been put into achieving those results along the way. In a test, those who study, practice and persevere will end up getting a better grade. In sports, an athlete who trains and lives a healthy lifestyle will achieve better results on the field. Those who invest in different areas of life will eventually succeed, because hard work and effort always come before results.

SO, WHAT ARE THE CODES?

They're a practical and simple way to implement a method for success in life. It's as simple as that!
This is your journey from your "You of Today", toward your "Greatest You"!

That is, from where you are today, in all the different areas of your life, toward greatness and success!

JOURNEY TOWARD YOUR
"GREATEST YOU"

TWO KEY CONCEPTS accompany the method: ACHIEVING and FULFILLMENT.

○ **Achieving is like science:** you have to understand what you want to achieve and how to do it. And yet, we bet there are situations where you get your desired results and you're not as happy as you thought you'd be.

○ **Fulfillment**, however, is where you can learn to feel good about yourself.

○ **Achieving and Fulfillment.** Combine these two important things. Imagine being able to say to yourself, "I know what I want to achieve for myself and how to do it, and I can feel good about myself when doing it".

○ **Success is not a fluke.** It is not something that happens by chance. You can't just sit and wait for it to happen to you. There's a clear and defined technique for success in life, which you'll learn in this book. Your main project is your life and we're going to show you how to ace that project!

My main PROJECT is MY LIFE!

You're probably thinking—yeah, right, as if anyone can succeed easily in life. While you might think you can't be the CEO of a big company, the inventor of something life-changing, or the President of the United States, without a doubt, with 100 percent certainty, you can be the best version of yourself possible. You can be a little better each day than you were yesterday. Your investment in reading this book is the best investment in yourself, because **you are giving yourself the greatest gift—a fast track to success**!

FAST TRACK TO SUCCESS

This book will quickly provide you with tools and skills which will prepare you for your life as an adult, in a competitive world that is rapidly changing.

In the future, you will engage in professions that may not even have been invented yet. That might sound crazy but that's why it's important for us to give you tools that will help you in whatever field you choose. No matter what you choose to pursue, which classes you choose to study, what subject you pick to major in (if you decide to go to college), where you'll pursue your higher education, etc. These tools and skills will serve you in the best way possible, at any age, at any stage and in any place and field you find yourself.

And what about your family, your parents? To be honest, they can read this book too if you decide you'd like them to. There's a short note at the end of this book addressed to them and we encourage discussion, so your family can support you in your goals, but again, that is totally up to you.

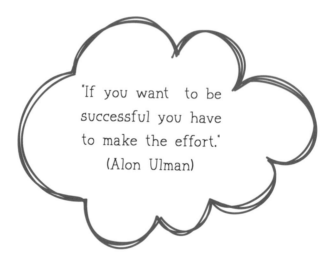

'If you want to be successful you have to make the effort.'
(Alon Ulman)

We always say, our students haven't changed, but the tools and skills they've learned from us have helped them toward their best versions of themselves! You're going to live in this world for many years to come. If you start applying the tools you'll learn in this book today, think how much easier it'll be for you when you're older and how amazing your results could be!

We used to think our method works; today we know it does because it achieves results. Tens of thousands of students have already reached extraordinary success and achievements in their lives.

Contrary to what people may think, your growth from the "You of Today" to your "Greatest You" never stops. Right now you're young and the tools and skills you'll learn in this book will allow you to continue your constant growth even when you're older. Each year you'll become better and more successful than you were in the previous year.

Our students are just like you! And now, it's your turn to be successful. All you have to do is read this book and apply yourself. We show you how and your half of the deal is to implement. You're signing an emotional contract with yourself to be the greatest "you" you can be! All the content in this book is presented in an easy-to-follow and practical way, to help you learn, understand and apply.

So, that's it—let's get started!

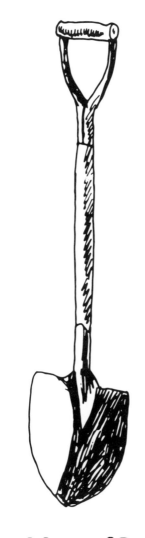

TOOLS FOR
SUCCESS

LET'S WATCH A MOVIE

Have you seen the movie *The Karate Kid*? There's also a newer version of it, but we mean the original movie from 1984. You weren't even born yet, but your parents probably remember it (ask them). It's a great movie and if you haven't seen it, we really recommend watching it. Make a big bowl of popcorn, invite some friends or family and watch it together. Movies can be a good way to make learning fun, so we recommend accompanying the movie with a viewing exercise (*see below*).

We hope you enjoyed the movie but for those who didn't watch, here's a short description of what happens:

Daniel, a teenage boy, moves to Los Angeles with his mother. Despite his attempts, he fails to make friends but falls in love with Ali, the former girlfriend of Johnny, the popular school bully. Daniel continues to get bullied by the popular kids but then he meets Mr. Miyagi, a master of martial arts and the superintendent in the building where Daniel lives. Mr. Miyagi takes Daniel under his wing, teaches him karate and helps him stick up for himself and finally face the bullies at school.

Another STEP FORWARD

WATCHING THE KARATE KID

If you decide to watch the movie, please answer the following questions while watching:

1. Who are the main characters in the movie?

2. What are the relationships between the main characters? (For example: Daniel and Lucille = mother and son).

3. How do the relationships change from the beginning of the movie to the end?

(For example: Daniel and Lucille = at the beginning of the movie Daniel is angry with his mother; at the end of the movie they have a good and loving relationship).

Think carefully: What's the main relationship in the movie?

The answer is clear. The relationship between Daniel and Mr. Miyagi is at the heart of the story! It's a wonderful example of a teacher-student relationship. For comparison, consider the differences between the teacher-student relationship of Mr. Miyagi and Daniel, and the teacher-student relationship of the other sensei and his students.

You're probably thinking, how does *The Karate Kid* relate to this book?

When Alon was a young officer in the Navy, his commander invited all the officers to a meeting. All the officers arrived, sat down and waited for the commander. When he arrived, he did not say a word to them. He entered the hall, played them a movie and sat quietly—and that movie was *The Karate Kid*, of course. When the movie ended, the commander stood up in the middle of the hall and shouted at the officers: "Do you understand?" and immediately left the room. So what did the commander want his officers to learn? What was his point?

The teacher's ADVANTAGE over the student: the TEACHER sees the BIGGER picture

In *The Karate Kid*, Mr. Miyagi gives Daniel different chores, like fixing things in his house and cleaning his car. Daniel isn't impressed with this because all he really wants to do is learn karate,  but now he's stuck doing all these jobs he doesn't like. In reality, Mr. Miyagi has been teaching Daniel karate moves all along, even when Daniel doesn't yet realize it, because the physical parts of the tasks he's been given are the movements that make up the very basics of karate.

We've all been in a class before where we've thought, "Why do I need to learn this?", right? Where we don't want to do the assignment because we don't understand why we're learning it in the first place. Here comes a very important lesson: the advantage of the teacher over the student. What does that actually mean? A good teacher, at every step of the way, knows where they want their students to end up and where they are leading them. The teacher understands the importance of basics, even when the student doesn't fully understand them yet. The basics students learn are the most important, until they become second nature and they can then move on to more complex teachings.

You might not realize why the assignment is important but your teacher knows it's valuable progress toward your success. A good teacher always sees the full picture, the final goal and knows exactly how to lead their students toward it, even before the students are able to understand that. The reason for this is quite simple; your teacher has already been down that road. They already went through it and have all the required experience ready to impart on to you.

The jobs Mr. Miyagi gave to Daniel are the ones that build his basics of karate. Mr. Miyagi knew what Daniel would achieve all along—long before Daniel understands this himself.

We, your mentors throughout this book, are those kinds of teachers. We also have a vision that is broader than yours right now when it comes to the codes in this book, and the tools and skills we are about to teach you. We also know exactly where this method will lead you in the future.

Please . . . trust us.

The teacher has the advantage over their students and there are two things to note here.

We will explain them easily using examples from *The Karate Kid*:

The first part is when Mr. Miyagi agrees to teach Daniel, and he tells him that if he walks on the right side of the road, or on the left side of the road, he will be fine—but if he walks in the middle of the road, he will be crushed like a grape. He is telling Daniel that he can choose whether to study karate or not to study karate, but he can't wing it, or it won't work.

The same applies for trusting that your teacher usually knows best. Either you will learn and complete every task that your teacher gives you properly, or you choose not to do anything. There is no halfway. This also applies for learning the codes. You either take this seriously, learning and applying the ten codes, or you don't do it at all. Winging it won't work! To summarize:

Whatever you do, do it well! This is your commitment to your own success! It's your commitment to the person who most influences your life: yourself!

The second thing to note is that a contract between the teacher and the student is formed. The student commits to do the things they are taught and that their teacher demands of them. At the same time, the teacher makes every effort to teach the student as best they can. In the movie, Daniel shakes hands with Mr. Miyagi and agrees to a binding contract between them. However, the second Mr. Miyagi tells him to clean his car, Daniel resists and starts asking questions until Mr. Miyagi reminds him of the commitment and the contract— the teacher has agreed to teach and the student has agreed to learn.

The same applies for the codes. Ask whatever you want about the material, but BE committed to act according to the ten codes in this book. As your teachers we see the bigger picture and we know that you will see results at the end of this process. You only have to be willing to learn.

This is your side of the contract between us. Be committed to your success!

THE METHOD

Your CHAMPION'S VISION

Here you'll learn to create the future you want. Think of all the things you dream about or can wish for yourself. Then you'll outline goals and targets and create the Champion's Vision in your reality.

Face your FEARS

You'll learn what is real and imaginary fear. You'll face failures and challenges, discover what holds you back and how you can overcome and get through that challenge. You'll reach a state where you're able to realize the Champion's Vision you have created for yourself. You'll learn how to operate in spite of fear and how to break boundaries.

CHAMPION behavior

You'll learn behaviors that, according to studies, make champions, and you will adapt these to use in your own life to achieve your goals. You'll learn how to maintain the achievements you have accomplished, and continue to act and behave like a champion.

THE RULES of SUCCESS

At the heart of this book are rules of success. They can be compared to the laws of nature, like gravity. You probably know that if you hold a pen in your hand and then let go, the pen will fall. Will this always happen? Maybe you should try again? Even if you try another 100 times, the result will be the same, because of gravity. From this you learn not to operate against gravity, because it's a rule of nature that always applies. There are such rules in the world of success and you'll learn them too.

"Everyone can achieve extraordinary results."

(Alon Ulman)

HOW DOES OUR METHOD WORK?

It's important to remember these four basic principles:

1. **Success is not a fluke.** Success of a person, an organization, a project, a business, a relationship, a soccer game, an election, in everything, is not a fluke. Success doesn't just happen.

2. **Anyone can achieve extraordinary results.** Most successful people weren't born like that. There's an actual method that teaches people how to get extraordinary results, if you're willing to put in the effort.

3. **You write the script of your life!** Even if you weren't aware of it until now. In a world of uncertainty people are constantly looking for a sign to show them what to do or tell them they're on the right path. This is the way the world has always been and it always will be. To be happy, we have a basic need for certainty. The big difference often found in successful people is that their certainty comes from

within they're the ones who write the script rather than those who depend on luck. When you realize you're the one writing your script, you're given personal leadership and personal responsibility for your life.

4. **You can learn how to succeed in life and take immediate control of your life.** In all fields, the basic understanding is that the person who most influences your life is you.

"They say that time does its thing. That's the point, it does its thing, it passes and passes. What we do while time is doing its thing will determine our success."

(Alon Ulman)

It might seem kind of obvious that all anyone wants in life is to be happy, healthy and successful, right? **So, if everyone wants to succeed, why isn't everyone successful?**

Why are there so many people who can't seem to make their dreams come true?

People have four main barriers to success:

1. They don't know the rules of success.

2. They don't know what they want to achieve.

3. They're too afraid and stop going after what they want.

4. They go back to old habits that haven't been helpful to them.

Don't worry, we're pretty sure you can get past these obstacles!

In this book you'll learn exactly how to overcome these barriers and move forward toward your goals!

As we mentioned earlier, all we ask is that you commit to the process, trust the process and trust us, and then you'll achieve results! Between us, why not give it a shot? The worst that could happen is that it ends up working.

It's important to remember that everyone progresses at their own pace. So, the progress in reading the book, taking action and in the results will also be different for each person. But, don't read the book, cross your fingers and say, "Oh, please let it happen to me". That won't work. **We're here to guide you through the whole process**, but you need to follow the codes, otherwise nothing will change.

It requires **active patience** from you. On the one hand, you have to be patient and understand that things take time, but on the other hand, you have to act according to the codes, set goals and targets and then act so you achieve them.

READY TO HIT THE ROAD?

Before going deeper, we need to mention something important. In this book , we don't have homework, we have **life lessons**! Life lessons are your part in putting the codes learned here into practice.

To achieve success and advance toward your "Greatest You", you need to put all ten codes of the book into your life. If you do this, you'll have the tools, skills and abilities to succeed. It can take time, but just remember to trust in the process.

The codes are a model for practical success. This book will accompany you for a long time and you can come back to it again and again, in various situations in your life and at different stages, as you grow older. A bit like a friend you can come back and get advice from whenever you need it. We'd love you to write your own thoughts and highlight the important things inside the book. Do whatever you feel can be helpful, in order to get the most out of this book.

The order of the codes doesn't matter as long as you put them all into action. We arranged them from number 1 through 10 just for your convenience. After reading and understanding the first code **you can read and use them in any order you choose**. You can read a chapter on a particular code, practice and make targets, and then move on to a chapter about a different code. You can also read all at once, or in any other way you see fit. You could even decide that your whole family will adopt one of the ten codes in the next month, working and focusing on it together, but we'll leave that up to you to decide.

The main thing is that you'll eventually read and put into action all ten codes. And that's it.

At the end of the book, you'll receive **a certificate of completion for studying this book**. We think this is one of the most important certificates you'll ever receive. Think about it, certificates are always given to us for our past accomplishments: what we have learned, what grade we got and so on. The certificate is special because it's a symbol of your future and the successes you'll have—as long as you continue to build on the skills you'll learn in these pages.

WHAT HAVE WE LEARNED?

YOUR MAIN PROJECT IS YOUR LIFE!

You're embarking on a journey from the "You of Today" to your "Greatest You"!

The codes are a practical and easy method to implement for success in life.

TRUST THE PROCESS

Trust the process. Learn the method and its basics because it works!

SUCCESS IS NOT A FLUKE

This book teaches practical success. You can learn it and take immediate control of your life.

Ordinary people can achieve extraordinary results.

WHATEVER YOU DO, DO IT WELL!

Read the book, learn the method and take it seriously!

You can learn to break down barriers in the way of your success because you make your own luck.

THE TEACHER'S ADVANTAGE OVER THE STUDENT.

We've been here before and we're here for you!

BE PATIENT AND PERSEVERE

Remember that each of us has a different pace of progress.

Code 2

Think Like a Champion

IDEA!

WHERE DO ALL YOUR RESULTS IN LIFE COME FROM ?

Wouldn't it be amazing if we knew exactly what was going on inside our brains? To find out, from a physiological or biological aspect, you'd need a good science book because that's not our specialty—but we can teach you how to be successful. We call this "thinking like a champion", and by doing so, we'll be able to answer lots of questions. Like, what motivates you? How can you control your thoughts, feelings and actions? These questions help manage your goals and expectations, so, in practice, if you learn to think like a champion you can manage your thoughts instead of letting your thoughts manage you.

So, Let's get to work! FOCUS, because this is IMPORTANT.

In order to think like a champion, there are four main components we need to look at. As we teach practical success, let's start and focus on the last stop— **the results**—so we can fully understand how we achieve results in life.

WHAT DO WE MEAN BY RESULTS?

Results are a consequence of a particular action. They can be desirable or undesirable.

Desired result = Success

Undesired result = Something you didn't want to happen

Let's go through a couple of examples:

Test score: a score in line with your goals is a desired result; a lower score than expected is an undesired result.

Relationships with family and friends: good relationships are the desired result; difficult relationships are the undesired result.

So, what do you THINK causes all the RESULTS in YOUR LIFE?

YOUR ACTIONS

Where do your **actions** come from? What actually motivates you to perform certain actions?

Actions are driven by our **emotions** and they can be divided into two groups. Negative emotions (such as jealousy, anger, hatred, sadness and so on); and positive emotions (such as love, affection, joy and so on).

Now, where do feelings come from?

YOUR THOUGHTS

We can also divide these into two groups: positive thoughts and negative thoughts. Each type of thought naturally leads to a different emotion.

Here we combine thoughts and emotions—the wisdom of the head and the wisdom of the heart in our inner world. Emotions are your emotional GPS (connecting to your emotions and what feels right to you). Thoughts are like a navigation system that guides us. The combination of the two and learning to think like a champion will lead to positive actions and the results you want.

Let's go through what you've learned.

Everything starts with thoughts,

which cause emotions,

which cause actions,

which cause results!

AND THIS CYCLE REPEATS ITSELF OVER AND OVER AGAIN!

As every result you get causes you to think again, the cycle never stops.

WE AS HUMANS CAN CONTROL TWO THINGS: OUR THOUGHTS AND OUR ACTIONS!

Thoughts cause emotions and actions cause results. So, if you succeed in controlling thoughts and actions, it will bring you the results you want, it's as simple as that!

LET'S LOOK AT SOME REAL-LIFE EXAMPLES

These are examples of students just like you. We will go step-by-step through how to change your usual thinking pattern and think like a champion instead. Imagine something we've all done—you woke up late and because you forgot to organize your school bag last night you're late for school.

What **thoughts** are going through your mind? Usually negative, right? "I'm late", "I probably forgot things at home", "My teacher's going to be mad", "Maybe I'll get a detention", etc.

What **emotions** will be triggered as a result of those thoughts? They're probably negative. Stress, panic, anger (probably not at yourself, but at your mom who forgot to wake you up, your younger brother who kept bugging you last night and made you forget to organize your bag, your annoying teacher), etc.

What **actions** will these emotions trigger? Most likely actions that are pretty unhelpful. You might try to explain and blame others, and your teacher will still think it's your fault for not taking personal responsibility for your actions. You might talk and interrupt the lesson since you don't have the relevant materials and books. Your classmates might get annoyed at you for interrupting the whole class and you might struggle with the lesson material because you missed some of it and didn't have your own stuff.

What **results** will these actions cause? To be honest, they wouldn't be great. You didn't have the required material for the lesson, you didn't listen properly in class because you were stressed, you disturbed your friends, you aggravated your teacher—you basically found yourself in an annoying situation you'd prefer not to be in.

Let's take another example. A student sits in a classroom and disturbs the entire class. Why are they doing that? For all sorts of reasons. Maybe they didn't bring the right equipment to the lesson, maybe they're bored and want to talk to their friend, maybe they don't understand the material and are struggling, so they've stopped trying. The student's thoughts are negative thoughts because they're not thinking about their success, they're just trying to make time pass in class. Their feelings are also negative, causing them to interrupt instead of paying attention. Who do you think they're bothering? The teacher, obviously. But it's also the other students in the class, who can't continue studying properly. They're also ruining their chance at understanding the material and learning. As a result, the class is unable to focus on the material being taught and the teacher is angry, and will probably punish the interrupting student. If the student is already struggling in class, they're not going improve their situation. As a result, they probably won't do well in the upcoming test or assignment.

You want another example? Here you go. A student arrives at school in the morning and realizes that one of the other students is talking about them. Their thoughts and emotions, as you can probably guess, are negative. They may choose a negative action, like doing the same thing back to that person, or starting a fight with them. The result is, of course, also negative. If they want to get reported to their teacher, the teacher will punish them, even if they say, "But I didn't start it". They know very well that it doesn't really matter who started it.

If you have come this far in the book, then you are a very intelligent person. You've probably already noticed that when we talk about thinking like a champion there are two parts to consider—a part that belongs to the inner world and a part that belongs to the outer world. Thoughts and emotions are internal, for all of us. No one can know what you're thinking or feeling unless you express this in an external way (for example, through smiling, laughing, or crying and so on). On the other hand, actions and results are external; others can know about them with the help of their senses (sight, hearing, touch, taste and smell) and they are in the external world.

MEET THE CHAMPION'S QUESTION!

Your main goal is to reach a state where you can ultimately choose your thoughts, influence the emotion and choose the actions and desired results for you. But we know that it's very difficult to do and it takes time and practice. Don't worry, it's also very difficult for adults.

In the meantime, we'll teach you to help yourself by managing actions.

So how do you DO THAT?
How do you CONTROL your MIND?

We'll train you to stop, just for a second, between the emotion and the action, right at the transition between the inner world and the outer world. Think of it as if you're building an imaginary wall, and you're making a stop between your emotions and your actions. This stop will help you choose the action that advances you toward the goals and targets you set for yourself!

During the second you stop before the action—before cursing, before getting angry at someone, before interrupting class, etc.—you ask yourselves **the Champion's Question:**

Does it ADVANCE ME?

THIS SIMPLE QUESTION IS VERY, VERY, VERY, VERY IMPORTANT!
With the help of this question, you create a space to stop between emotions and actions, and prevent yourself from doing something that will only add unwanted results to your life!

Using the Champion's Question, "Does it advance me?", gives you a **glimpse into your future**! Just like that. We don't have the ability to create a time machine, but that space, that little stop and that question allows you to sneak a peek into the future and see the result you're going to get following the action. This way you can choose whether to perform the action or not.

You're probably asking, "Advancing who and where?" The answer: does the action you're going to take **advance you**? Where? Toward the **result you wish to have for yourself**. In Code 10, the Champion's Questions, we'll talk about this more and ask whether this question can also help those around us.

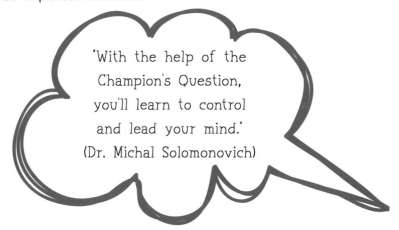

"With the help of the Champion's Question, you'll learn to control and lead your mind."
(Dr. Michal Solomonovich)

WiLL the ACTiON I take ADVANCE ME toward MY GOALS?

Do you think only young people can benefit from thinking like a champion? What about adults? Of course, it works exactly the same for young people and adults. However, the sooner you learn and the younger you are when learning it, the better it'll be for you.

Let's go back to the stories we spoke about earlier. Let's try to see how the young people could have acted differently and stopped the actions that led to negative results. **What would have happened if they had stopped for a second and asked themselves, "Does it advance me?"**

In the first example, we told you about the student sitting in the classroom and interrupting the lesson. Same as earlier, they are experiencing negative thoughts and emotions. But this time they'll pause for a second and ask themselves the Champion's Question: does interrupting in class advance me?

It's easy to assume they'll understand that the answer is no. After all, they're disturbing their own learning. They definitely don't want a detention or a bad grade. They're annoying the other students in the class and the teacher who's just trying to do their job. When they behave this way it just leads to an angry teacher and falling behind in class.

However, this time, the student will understand that before taking that step they can choose another course of action that advances them more. For example, they could tell the teacher that they're experiencing difficulties with the material and ask them to explain it to them again.

The teacher will be much more willing to help them if they know the student is eager to understand.

ANOTHER STEP FORWARD.

Our ultimate goal is to help you control some of your negative thoughts. That's not easy, we know. However, one step at a time, after many times of applying this method in different situations in your life it'll become natural for you.

At the point where you're in the first stage of the inner world, at the time of choosing your thoughts, start asking yourself the question, "Does it advance me?". Then you can start sorting your thoughts into one of two categories: those that advance you and those that do not. Does a particular thought advance you or not? This will allow you to stop yourself from choosing the non-advancing thoughts and focus on those that do advance you. Eventually, you'll be able to program the thoughts in the inner world to act according to that question. There'll be no need to wait for the stop between emotions and actions—you'll already be able to do this at an earlier stage.

As a result, in the next test or paper, the student's chances of success will be much better. The same applies in the example of the students gossiping. The kid who got hurt has negative thoughts and emotions, but this time they build a wall and stop for a second before taking action. If they ask themselves whether it advances them to continue the gossip and argue, they'll realize that it can only lead to a negative result for them. The best approach would be to calmly try to talk to the other student, to ignore and walk away, or go to their teacher.

Always USE the COMPASS of SUCCESS!

Another tool that could help you answer the important question "Does it advance me?" is the personal Compass of Success!

Your personal Compass of Success—you're the only one who can really adjust it, because it's part of you. You get to decide if you want your personal compass to point in the direction of success or in the direction of failure. A compass should always point north, toward your goals.

Two IMPORTANT RULES for operating the COMPASS:

1. **Champions go out on the field to win.** Some people tell themselves in advance that they can't win. There are students who come to school and want to make the best out of it, socially, academically, etc. They want to win, even if they don't always manage it. Sometimes you'll succeed and sometimes you won't, but the intention is always to do the best you can. Others hope they don't lose and tell themselves it's enough. But in a football game, those who go out on the field to win have direction and an achievement in sight. They've set their thinking to achieve the most they possibly can and that makes a big difference.

To operate the COMPASS of SUCCESS, you need to know what SUCCESS MEANS for YOU.

2. **To adjust the compass you need to have a clear definition of what success means to you.** You must ask yourself, as a champion, what will be considered in your eyes as a win, and you must have a clear and precise definition. For example, at the start of the school year, ask yourself, "What would be considered a victory at the end of the school year?" Already, just by asking this question, you'll be able to turn your entire school year into a more positive year.

The CHAMPION'S METHOD for defining the DESIRED RESULT from end to BEGINNING!

Champions ask themselves, "What will be considered a success?" It's very important in the beginning to define the desired goal you want to achieve at the end. It's never too early to think about what result you want to see in the future. Then go back to your thoughts and decide what actions you can perform today. These actions will help you advance and reach your goal in the future.

The more times you use the personal Compass of Success and ask the Champion's Question, the more you will practice controlling positive and negative thoughts.

Something that will help with positive thoughts is a **list of successes**. Take a piece of paper, or the last page in your notebook or diary, and write down a success that you have experienced today. You can add to this every day, small successes, big successes, all successes. We know that at first you'll probably have a hard time finding something to write. You might think you had no successes today or that you're not good at anything. So, let's start together. Take a pen now (yes, right now!) and write three successes from the last month. It can be literally anything: a grade you were happy with, a compliment someone gave you, a fun day with one of your friends, doing well at a computer game, etc. Literally any success that comes to mind. Then put the notebook next to your bed, or stick the page over your desk in your bedroom, and update it every day. You will very quickly discover what we already know—you are successful. The only problem you have is that sometimes you don't see these successes, because it's very easy to focus on negative things.

We BELIEVE that everyone should SEE the GOOD in THEMSELVES.

Please make writing in the list of successes an everyday task. We assure you that the first page will fill up very quickly and you'll end up needing to add more and more pages to the list. Also, please don't throw them away. Keep them so you can look through them. There is nothing more enjoyable than looking through the list as it grows longer! We also think you'll be amazed at how quickly the question "Does it advance me?" will save you from actions and results you'll regret later.

We know you're a student, whether you're home-schooled or go to an actual school building every day, so we have created a special checklist that will help you remember the important things. Although, these can be applied in all areas of your life, not just in your schoolwork. This checklist will help navigate your personal Compass of Success toward your goals.

NAVIGATE
TOWARD YOUR
GOALS

○ PREPARE
Be prepared for any opportunity that comes your way.

○ ARRIVE ON TIME
As we mentioned earlier, you can't get the most out of something if you're missing it.

○ WHATEVER YOU DO, DO IT WELL!
Always! That doesn't necessarily mean you'll always get 100 on a test, but the best you can do. Be thorough and focus on your actions by setting yourself goals and targets.

There is more about this in Code 6. Be in a constant and permanent state of growth on the journey from the "You of Today" to your "Greatest You"! So that every day you can be a little better than you were yesterday.

○ TAKE ACTION
You can only make something materialize by acting on it.

○ PERSEVERE
Sometimes you won't get your desired result straight away, but nothing worth having comes easily, right?

○ FRIENDSHIPS AND RELATIONSHIPS

Aspire to have relationships where cooperation, teamwork and supporting each other feel second nature. You have to give everything you want from the universe back into the universe, so be the kind of friend, family member or teammate you want to have.

○ WRITE YOUR OWN SCRIPT! YOU ARE THE DIRECTOR OF YOUR LIFE!

You are writing your script, whether you're aware of it or not. You determine what is success and what is failure in your life. You're responsible for your choices. You're the one asking and answering the question "Does it advance me?"

○ REMEMBER, THE ONLY PLACE WHERE THE WORD "SUCCESS" COMES BEFORE THE WORD "WORK" IS IN THE DICTIONARY!

In real life, you can't get anything in exchange for nothing. You have to take action and put in the work. We hope you'll soon see how good it feels to put in the effort and invest in yourself. When you're looking after yourself properly it can only lead to success!

THE DIRECTOR OF YOUR LIFE

YOU LEAD YOURSELF!!!

"I am the director of my life" is a rule that stems from **personal leadership and personal responsibility**.

PERSONAL LEADERSHIP

If you're not able to lead yourself, you won't be able to lead others.

PERSONAL RESPONSIBILITY

If you want to get the results you want in life, you realize that you must act out of personal responsibility. This is your life and you are the one taking responsibility.

So, think of yourself as a movie director. The role of the director in a movie is the most important. They determine what the movie will look like, how the actors should say their lines, etc. Since we're actually talking about your life, think of yourself not only as the director, but also as the lead actor, the producer, the costume designer, and the screenwriter. In fact, most of the roles are yours, because this is the movie of your life.

You're the one writing the script in your movie. Now you know how to think like a champion, you'll be able to create the best movie possible.

Which would you prefer? For your life to be a Hollywood blockbuster, or a B-movie broadcast at 2am on some remote TV channel?

We think we know the answer!

So, imagine yourself sitting in a glorious director's chair, directing the new blockbuster movie:

The Life of —————— ———————!! (Just add your name)

You're the one writing your movie, so you should be the person holding the pen. (Of course, that's just a metaphor, today we mostly type everything .)

When you find yourself in a situation where you act without thinking, you're unable to stop in that moment between emotions and actions— and that means you're no longer the one holding the pen. You're not the one writing your script! This means you're practically (whether you want to admit it or not) handing over the control of your life and the writing of your script, to another person. Can you be sure that that person has your best interests at heart and they're not acting out of their own personal interest? Of course not. Only you can write the best script for your life.

Don't pass the pen to someone else!

I'M THE DIRECTOR OF MY LIFE

Create a movie clapperboard to show you're the director of your life. You can name your movie whatever you want!

DIRECTOR OF YOUR LIFE

MY PERSONAL
COMPASS OF SUCCESS

Create a sign that says, "My Compass of Success", with the Champion's Question "Does it advance me?".

Hang the sign in your room or keep it somewhere that'll remind you of the Champion's Question every time you look at it.

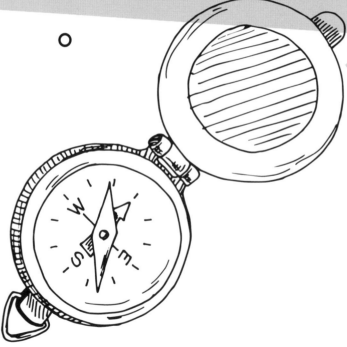

WHAT HAVE WE LEARNED?

WHERE DO ALL YOUR RESULTS IN LIFE COME FROM?
Thoughts—Emotions—Actions—Results.

YOU CAN LEARN TO CONTROL YOUR OWN THOUGHTS AND ACTIONS
The Champion's Question: "Does it advance me?"

START A LIST OF YOUR SUCCESSES
In order to write your own script, you need to be the one holding the pen.

USE YOUR COMPASS OF SUCCESS AND CHECKLIST TO LEAD YOU TO YOUR GOALS
The importance of leadership and personal responsibility because you are the director of your life.

Code 3

You Have to Climb a Lot of Stairs on the Way to Success

QUESTIONS FOR SELF-REFLECTION

What is the opposite of success? Think hard before you answer.

The chances are, you answered that failure is the opposite of success. Don't worry, you're in good company —the first time we ask most people this question they've answered with failure. But this answer is really, really wrong!

FAILURE IS PART OF THE ROAD TO SUCCESS!

Failure means **getting an undesired result**. That's all.

In this code we'll teach you to act in a special method we call **Failing Forward**.

ALL SUCCESSFUL people experience DIFFICULTIES.

We want you to realize that it's really okay and part of the path to the next level. On the road to success it's natural and normal that some things won't work out, and letting that stop you is a mistake! If you don't try, you can't learn. The idea of Failing Forward is vital because it's an idea built on the basic understanding that stumbling blocks aren't the opposite of success, but rather a part of it.

Everyone experiences obstacles. It's impossible to always skip from one success to the other without having to pick yourself up occasionally when things don't work out. A champion accepts each of these moments as a lesson for next time. Each one is an opportunity to explore, learn, understand what went wrong, what not to do and how to improve for next time. These are the most important lessons in life.

Consider each FAILURE as a step that advances you FORWARD TOWARD your GROWTH and DEVELOPMENT.

Failure is something you can learn from, that can strengthen you and teach you how to be more focused on your goals and targets. **Failure means not getting the result you wanted. That's all.**

REMEMBER: ALL SUCCESSFUL people have experienced OBSTACLES before their SUCCESS.

You'll fall and experience challenges before succeeding. The only difference will be how you choose to respond to this.

Do you have any younger siblings or babies in your family? You must have seen how babies start to learn to walk. What happens to them? Do they manage to stand on their feet and walk safely the first time they try? Of course not! Babies fall over and over again, until they learn to walk.

And what about the parents? Have you ever seen a mom or dad tell their baby not to try again after they've fallen? Of course not! The parents are there to encourage their baby to try again and again and not give up. No matter how long it takes them, the baby and parents will keep going until the baby learns how to walk.

For some reason, as we get older, we forget this and stop trying as hard because we're afraid to fail.

Why do the parents continue to encourage their baby? Because the end result is clear to them and they know their child will walk. They don't consider another option because they're confident their child will succeed.

So, from now on, remember that baby, and no matter what happens, no matter how many times you fail on the way to your goal, you will keep going on and on! This is the basis of the Failing Forward method.

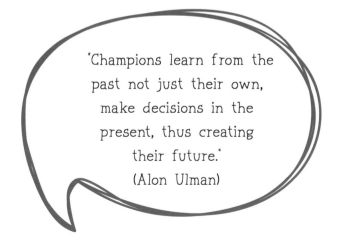

"Champions learn from the past not just their own, make decisions in the present, thus creating their future."
(Alon Ulman)

No matter what goal or target you choose – it could be becoming a professional basketball player, or performing in a dance show, or getting a high grade on a math test – the list goes on. The achievement isn't relevant right now to set your thinking to Failing Forward mode. Whatever goal or target you choose, your thinking must be like that of the baby learning to walk. The thing that applied to you, when you were a little baby and learned how to walk, is relevant throughout your whole life.

Even if you've failed, you just got an undesired result. You go on, examine what happened, learn the lesson, develop a new ability if needed and do it again until you get the desired result.

That doesn't mean you don't have to do anything. After all, if you sit in class, cross your fingers and hope you pass your English test it won't help toward your success. You have to work for it.

You can't get anything in this world without contributing. You have to make a deliberate effort, a decision, or collection of decisions that direct you toward your desired goal.

Part of that action is Failing Forward. There isn't a single person who's managed to avoid failure in their life.

DON'T LET GO OF YOUR DREAMS

Everyone experiences disappointment. The difference between a champion and the rest is that most people just cross their fingers and wait for something to happen to them, while a champion applies the Failing Forward approach. They don't give up. They don't let go of their dream. They go again and again until they succeed.

Failing Forward means that you have to be willing to take a first step many times, even if it is scary. Walking forward takes us out of our comfort zone and symbolizes our growth. It is very important that you move outside of your comfort zone and experience the failures that come with the road to success.

What if it doesn't work?

Young people always ask us this question. It's a question that holds most people back and prevents them from trying again. Our answer is very simple: there's no guarantee in success and we can't tell you the number of times you'll have to fall and get up to reach your target.

PEOPLE want guarantees in SUCCESS and there is NO SUCH THING!

There's a very simple answer to this: if it doesn't work, then it doesn't work.

That's it.

There's no great and successful person who hasn't failed several times on the path to success. Sometimes the failures are very unpleasant. The important thing is that champions know the **special definition of success**:

SUCCESS = one, plus the number of failed attempts you made on the way to your goal. So, if you failed twice and tried three times, that is a success. Usually, this definition reassures most kids, because success is no longer something big, unreachable and scary. Success is simply about trying again and again and again, just one more time than the number of attempts we have failed until you succeed!

Ordinary people: either fail or succeed.

Champions: fail, fail, fail, fail before achieving success.

The conclusion is clear: you can't give up on yourself when it comes to making your big dreams come true. No one wants failure, but with the help of the Failing Forward method, you can learn how to cope when you don't get the result you wanted and move forward until you learn to walk!

It's important to REMEMBER you must be separate from YOUR ACTIONS.

FAILURE DOESN'T REFLECT ON YOU, BUT A SEQUENCE OF ACTIONS.

If you change your actions, you'll eventually achieve your goal! If you fail, it simply means that the actions you took were unsuccessful. But that doesn't mean that you, as a person, aren't successful. If you get a low score on a test it means that your actions led to the situation where you deserved that low score, not that you're worth that score.

Looking at things from this perspective will help you avoid fear of failure and map out a way to reach your goals.

Kids often ask us, "Why do successful people always seem to have a difficult life story?" But, of course, this isn't really the case. We like hearing high achievers talk about the struggles they went through and how they overcame them to lead a happy and successful life. These people have used the Failing Forward method and refused to give up until they reached their goals. Everyone experiences difficulties, but champions use their failures to grow, then they dust themselves off and take action.

HOW SERIOUS ARE YOU ABOUT ACHIEVING YOUR TARGET?

THOSE WHO DON'T GIVE UP, SUCCEED, BIG TIME

Think of someone you admire. They can be from any industry you want: sports, music, games: the possibilities are endless. Maybe this person also has a difficult life story, and if they do it's very likely that they overcame lots of setbacks along their path to success. The difference between them and many others, is that this person never gave up.

Champions finish the race. Always. The right way is to focus on your goal and finish what you started. Think again about the baby who wants to learn to walk. They won't stop until they reach the goal, finish the race and learn to walk. They continue to operate according to the Failing Forward method. How long? As long as needed! They don't stop until they finish!

CHAMPIONS **FINISH** THE RACE

So why doesn't everyone BECOME A CHAMPION? Why can't some people FINISH THE RACE?

First of all, people often have lots of unhelpful habits. One big one is arriving late!

You have to go to all sorts of places: school, meetings, the movies, family events and so on. Think for a second, do you always arrive on time? Be real. We're pretty sure the answer's no.

Champions are never late, of course—but they also don't arrive on time.

If you start changing your habit by arriving at school just a little bit earlier, you'll immediately see how that will change your day. You'll have time to talk to your friends before class. You can check you've got everything you need for your day and will avoid starting your day stressed out. Just give it a try tomorrow morning, leave the house 15 minutes before you usually leave and you'll see how that will change your day!

Champions who arrive ahead of time usually need to use Failing Forward less, because some of the problems and failures they used to have were because of them being late all the time. This doesn't just apply to school, but sports training, meeting with a friend, etc. Think of a grown-up being late for work every day—up to what point will their boss tolerate that behavior? Eventually they'll get fired because they're showing that they're not serious about their job.

You want to show everyone—your parents, teachers, friends— that you're serious and reliable.

"CHAMPIONS DON'T ARRIVE ON TIME, they arrive AHEAD of time!"

(Dr. Michal Solomonovich)

YOU ARE A REAL CHAMPION!

So, it's been decided, tomorrow morning you'll arrive at school a little earlier. Deal? If you make that promise it's important to understand that you're not making the promise to us but to yourself.

Now let's learn another rule, which is very important on the road to success—**the 10,000 rule**.

A person who wishes to become an expert in their field, needs to give 10,000 hours of practice in that field. **You can't succeed without giving something**. Imagine if you practiced every day for about 90 minutes in the thing you wanted to master. Within ten years you could accumulate plenty of hours of experience and be incredible!

Take, for example, Michael Jordan—the most influential basketball player of all time. When he was young, his coach sat him on the bench, even though he was the best player on the team. The coach told Michael he was undisciplined and wouldn't succeed, because the natural talent he had wasn't enough. For a long time, Michael didn't play, even though the team lost, and the coach told him he would only bring him back when he'd learned how to be a team player. Michael eventually realized he had to change his ways. He would come to practice an hour earlier and leave an hour later. He trained harder than anyone. Michael has said on several occasions that he owes his career to this coach. Unfortunately, lots of us aren't lucky enough to have a person like this to take us under their wing and help.

And that is EXACTLY why WE'RE HERE FOR YOU!

In order to illustrate the 10,000 rule, think of a kid who's learning to play the piano or basketball, they could even be learning to dance, or studying to improve their math. Every year they get better and better because they've invested the hours needed to reach the level or goal they've set for themselves.

"Achieving against myself is far more important than achieving in competition with others!"
(Dr. Michal Solomonovich)

We want you to look at this rule in another way. Instead of 10,000 hours, there's 10,000 **attempts**. Remember Thomas Edison? He's the guy who invented the lightbulb. He said something very famous:

"I did NOT FAIL, I just found 10,000 WAYS that did NOT WORK."

And that is exactly the way of thinking we want you to adopt. It matches the Failing Forward method we discussed earlier.

Let's tell you another story about James Dyson, the inventor and owner of the global vacuum cleaner company Dyson. Their rechargeable wireless models that can be used to vacuum the entire house without connection to an outlet are very popular today, and are used in many homes around the world. At the beginning, Dyson wanted to create a vacuum that didn't use a bag inside to collect dust—which is now the norm today because of him—and it took 5,127 attempts to get the right prototype and create the world's first bagless vacuum cleaner.

Think what would have happened if he were to stop after a couple of attempts, after 20, 100, 1,518? But he didn't stop or give up: he acted with determination following the Failing Forward method.

Now imagine yourself trying to solve a difficult math problem. How many times do you really try to solve it? Once, twice, three times? Maybe five if you're really giving it your best. And that's it, then you give up and move on to the next exercise. In class, you tell your teacher that you couldn't do it.

We want to teach you that until you've tried 5,127 times, or even 10,000 times, you absolutely can't give up!

This is the big difference between champions and others: **never give up—because you'll never know how close you were!**

You are a CHAMPION when you achieve the GOALS set for YOURSELF! (And not in competition.)

How many champions are there in a competition? Usually one, right? Sometimes, when it comes to sports, there are three winners: a gold, a silver and a bronze medal. But there are usually 30 – 35 students in a class, sometimes even more. If you act in class like you would in a competition, there'll be one champion, maybe three.

And what ABOUT EVERYONE ELSE?

This is exactly why you need to change the way you think and realize you're not in a competition, not when you're in class or anywhere else. You become a champion in achieving. **Achieving** means you don't need to compare yourself to anyone except yourself. This means that every day you're a little better than you were yesterday—and that's when you become a real champion.

Let's take an example at school. If you scored higher in your recent English test than your previous test then you won. You progressed in comparison to yourself—so you're a true champion! When this happens you need to celebrate and be proud of yourself, and be happy with the process and progress you're making!

This applies to every area of your life and not just school. If you shift your way of thinking, this will also help you be happy for others and for others to be happy for you in return. When there's no more comparison and competition, we can all be champions!

Of course, we know that there are exceptions to the rule. There will always be kids who try to take you down. In these kinds of situations, you need to be strong, lead by example, remember all the things you've learned here and ignore the bad behavior. Being overly competitive doesn't help you and it doesn't help them! If you ever lose faith in yourself, search for a **supportive environment**, your family or friends will be there for you. And, of course, always remember that **your past is not a sign of your future**—even if you have failed in the past, it doesn't mean failure in the future.

WE CAN ALL BE CHAMPIONS!

I CAN FAIL FORWARD!

Think about the code of Failing Forward and how we win when we persevere. Make a poster of all the different ways you could attempt a goal you would like to achieve. We bet you can think of at least ten!

FAILURE ISN'T THE OPPOSITE OF SUCCESS —IT'S PART OF IT

Write about an area of your life where you succeeded but hit some bumps along the road. Explain how you got over them.

CHAMPION HEROES

Choose someone you admire (this could be a famous person, a historic person, someone from your close family, etc.) and look at how they became a success. Did they encounter bumps along the road? How do you think they overcame these?

FAILING FORWARD

Write down something you worked hard to improve in your life and divide it according to the catapult. Here's an example:

Starting point: I got a D in my biology test.

Middle point: I asked my teacher for extra help.

End point: In the next test I got a B.

WHAT HAVE WE LEARNED?

CHAMPION'S THOUGHT

You learn from the past, make decisions in the present, so you create your future.

No one wants to fail, but it's a normal part of the path to success.

FAILING FORWARD

Failure doesn't reflect on you, but a series of actions change the actions and you will succeed!

CHAMPIONS FINISH THE RACE

Champions arrive ahead of time.

THE 10,000 RULE

You become a champion through your achievements and not through competition.

Don't give up because you'll never know how close you were.

Your past is not an indication of your future!

BECOME A CHAMPION
THROUGH YOUR ACHIEVEMENTS

Code 4

Your Thoughts Create Your Reality

"IT'S all IN YOUR HEAD."

(Dr. Michal Solomonovich)

HOW TO CREATE THOUGHTS THAT GENERATE RESULTS

Remember the Disney Pixar movie *Inside Out?* The main character was a girl named Riley, and inside her head were characters who represented different emotions: joy, fear, anger, sadness, and disgust. Inside her head was also a control panel that made her feel different emotions. At the end of the movie, Riley learns that she controls what goes on in her head and her own actions. So, we know that it's really all in your head.

THOUGHTS REALLY DO CREATE YOUR REALITY!

Another STEP FORWARD

Information: everything it's possible to know, a collection of facts and data.

Knowledge: everything you know and are familiar with.

Awareness: your realization of the existence of something.

Consciousness: your understanding of your reality. Your ability to understand the relationship between your personal identity and the world you live in.

Do you know the **rice "experiment"**? It's a famous activity that's fun to do at home. Although it hasn't been scientifically proved, it illustrates the concept "your thoughts create your reality" really well! Here's how to do it.

O You cook white rice (with the help of a parent!).

O You take two small glass jars. You put the same amount of cooked white rice in the jars (two or three spoons will do) and close them.

O On one jar you put a sticker with the word "love" on it and on the other jar you put a sticker with the word "hate".

O You put the jars on the counter in your kitchen, keeping them apart from each other. Every day for one month, you stand by the love jar and say positive things to the rice. Lots of kind, joyful words.

O Then you stand by the hate rice jar and say negative things to the rice. You can be as horrible as you like.

O What do you think will happen? Do you think there'll be a difference between the rice jars? Or do you think they'll stay the same?

Our People who did this activity reported that after a few days, the rice in the love jar was still white and it looked almost good enough to eat. While the rice in the hate jar had started to grow mold and go black. There are tons of videos online that show the experiment and its results, just search "rice experiment" on YouTube and take a look. Whether you think the rice experiment would work or not, how about we look at it another way? Imagine how you would feel if someone said positive things to you every day. You would probably start to feel more confident and happier, right? Well, compare this to how you would feel if someone said negative things to you all the time. The message here is clear:

Thoughts create reality!

Your THOUGHTS and WORDS have TREMENDOUS POWER!

Your energy goes into everything around us and the effects are deeper than we can imagine.
We can sum it up in a couple of sentences:

Think positively and you'll advance in life.
Think negatively and you'll hold yourself back.

That is the power of your mind!

And here's another example:

In the year 1968, two American researchers, Rosenthal and Jacobson, performed an experiment in different places in the US. The experiment is known as the "**Rosenthal Effect**" and also as the "**Pygmalion Effect**". The experiment illustrated that thoughts can create reality, like a **self-fulfilling prophecy**. The researchers showed in their research how false information about a student's abilities can impact the expectations of the teachers and parents of that student, and even the expectation of the student themselves and the results this students has achieved.

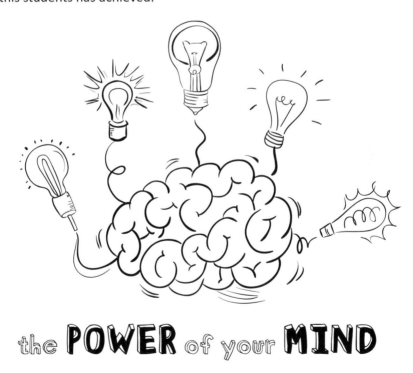

the POWER of your MIND

During the experiment, researchers came to different schools and gave an IQ test to every student. But instead of checking the tests, the researchers randomly selected students from each class and declared them as the ones who did best. These students were defined as being particularly gifted with a higher chance for success.

After a few days, the researchers returned to the schools and revealed the names of the gifted students to the teachers. At the end of the year, data was collected and showed that the students defined as gifted had improved more than the other children.

Why did this happen? The study showed that if teachers were led to expect great results, the students performed better. So performance can be influenced (good or bad) by the expectations of others.

If people believe in you, your self-esteem is boosted and you're more likely to believe that you're capable of great things. Now do you see what we mean when we say it's all in our heads?

Remember how it works: Thoughts—Emotions—Actions—Results.

In order for a thought to become reality, you need to act on it!

The children who participated in the experiment weren't satisfied with just thinking and believing that they have special abilities. Thinking they were gifted made them take action until a reality improvement was created.

Your expectation of yourself creates your greatness.

You too have the ability to be a high achiever!

What do you think? Do you believe us now when we say that everything's in your head and that thought creates reality?

As far as we know, each and every one of you reading this book has **the ability to be a high achiever** in every aspect of your life. You don't really need us to come to your class and conduct a study for that to be true, so please, truly believe in yourself and your abilities!

We want you to write the following sentence in a notebook and sign it. It's your promise to believe in yourself:

"I, _____ have the ability to be a high achiever"

_____

Signature

So, now that you know you can succeed, you need to change your way of thinking. Your self-image is essential to your success!

It doesn't really matter what others think of you. The important thing is what you think of yourself.
The journey spoken about at the beginning of this book, from the "You of Today" to your "Greatest You", is mainly based on your own self-belief. Your progress toward your "Greatest You" is made possible because of you!

You can be a greater version of yourself every passing day!

THINK POSITIVE

GOODNIGHT RITUAL

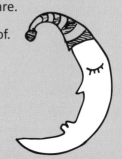

○ Always remember how smart and talented you are.

○ Never let anyone tell you what you are capable of.

○ Whatever you do, do it well.

○ You can be anything you want to be.

○ Never give up on your dreams.

○ No matter what happens, always remember how much you're loved.

As of today, the paragraph above will be part of your goodnight ritual.

Every night, when you are already in bed and right before falling asleep, read this to yourself, out loud if possible. You can even invite someone in your family to join you for this ritual.

Why it's IMPORTANT to read before going TO SLEEP?

Before falling asleep, alpha wave activity rises in your brain, allowing your subconscious to pick up messages. As we have established, thought creates reality and we want your subconscious to absorb all the important messages in this goodnight ritual. We want you to nurture your belief in yourself and really change your way of thinking.

Remember Mr. Miyagi in *The Karate Kid*? The method he used to teach Daniel karate was different and special because he taught and Daniel followed without asking questions. So, this is exactly the same, here is the place to do what we say, no questions asked. We also explained you the reasons.

Please perform this goodnight ritual every night before going to bed. It'll really help your self-belief, and you'll be able to see how positive thought helps make good things come true!

To understand how thoughts create reality, we want you to imagine an apple tree.

External world: above the surface.
Inner world: below the surface.

If you want to have beautiful and delicious apples grow on the tree, where should you water them? Is it at the top of the tree where the apples grow? You probably already know that's wrong. We need to water the roots so the water nourishes the entire tree—only then will apples grow.

And if you were to pick one apple from the tree, or all the apples, would the tree die? No, of course not. The tree will be able to grow new apples. It's only when the roots are damaged that the tree will die.

WHAT ABOUT HUMAN ROOTS?

Where do humans need to be "watered" in order for them to grow and flourish?

YOU LIVE IN
FOUR WORLDS

THE INNER WORLD:

MENTAL WORLD

Your thoughts.

THE EMOTIONAL WORLD

Your emotions.

THE SPIRITUAL WORLD

Your beliefs that motivate you and values you believe in.

THE OUTER WORLD:

THE PHYSICAL WORLD

Your body and everything that is in the tangible world. It's the world you spend most time in. It's the only one that is visible and your five senses—sight, hearing, touch, smell and taste—operate in it.

An investment in YOUR INNER WORLDS will bring you RESULTS in the OUTER WORLD.

Each of these worlds exists within us and together they create a whole person.

In order to simplify it, let us look at it like a circle divided into four quarters. Each world makes up 1/4 of the circle. Meaning, the external, physical, world is only 1/4 of the circle. And 3/4 of the circle is made up of the inner worlds—your thoughts, beliefs and emotions. The whole circle, and you, are made up of all four worlds together.

The division is between the outer world (the physical—what you are able to see with your eyes) and the inner worlds (your thoughts, emotions and beliefs—what you aren't able to see with your eyes).

The tree is, of course, a metaphor.

The apples, represent the results of human beings in the physical world. Similar to a test score, or a nice shirt, or good friendships, etc.

Unfortunately, most people only see the fruit (or their results) and if the fruit isn't tasty they blame the tree.

What do THEY FAIL to SEE?

They fail to see what is happening below the surface in the inner world (or the roots of the tree).

People usually invest most of their time and work in the external, physical world, where they can use the five senses. They ignore or forget about their inner worlds and that's a big mistake. The fruit is the end result of a great investment, they don't realize that under the surface, the roots of the tree need to be strong for the tree to be stable and withstand storms.

This is similar to a 20-story building. The foundations need to be carefully laid for them to be able to carry the weight of the building.

The main thing you need to remember is that you first need to invest in your inner world. Deepen your roots. You can't try to change from the outside and expect the change to really happen—it has to come from the inside as well.

Your roots need to be watered and nurtured like the roots of a tree for you to grow, advance and evolve. If you take care of the inner worlds, this will eventually be reflected in the outer world in your results.

One of the great ways to water your roots is **to work on your personal development**. The fact that you are reading this book shows that your growth is important to you and that you are invested in this. Life in the four worlds shows that thought really does create reality! If you work on your inner worlds, the results will appear in reality, in the outer physical world!

A relatively well-known question in relation to the inner world versus the outer world:

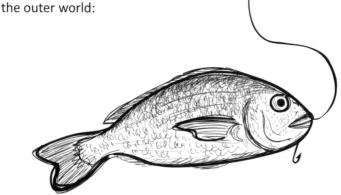

WHICH IS BETTER TO GIVE A HUNGRY PERSON–A FISH OR A FISHING ROD?

If they're given a fish, they'll eat it and won't be hungry. But what will happen in a few hours? They'll be hungry again and then there's no more fish to give them. On the other hand, if they're given a fishing rod, they will gain a lot more in the long run. It will take them longer to catch the first fish and eat it, but by then they'll already have the knowledge and ability to catch more fish and they won't have to go hungry anymore, because they'll be able to fish anytime they want.

So, which is better to give to a hungry person? A fish or a rod? You probably already know the answer.

SUCCESS IS NOT ALWAYS WHAT YOU SEE.

HIGH ENERGY ALWAYS WINS

Your energy can easily affect your thoughts, and as a result, your reality, whether you are getting up every morning with high energy or starting your day on low energy.

Unless you decide to change, how you act now is going to be the way you always behave. It's so easy to put off change and make excuses. You may not feel like studying seriously now or listening in class. It's easy to say you'll begin next week or in the next class. Change is hard, but you need to put the effort in today if you want to be better tomorrow.

There are many ways to increase your energy: dancing, exercising, setting yourself goals that excite you, music.

WRITE POSITIVE AFFIRMATIONS

WHAT ARE AFFIRMATIONS?

Affirmations are **positive statements** that are spoken in the present tense, as if they are happening now. Affirmations have an effect when repeated over and over again. They greatly affect our self-image and self-confidence. Remember what we said before—thought really does create reality!

INCREASE YOUR ENERGY

MY PERSONAL
AFFIRMATIONS

Please write down your personal affirmations. It can be one sentence that you want to say to yourself every day when looking in the mirror. A sentence that reflects what you feel, understand, think, believe—something that could change your way of thinking and make your thoughts a reality in the physical world! Say this sentence every morning, in the mirror and believe it!

For example: Today I am having a great day!

Saying positive affirmations raises your energy levels. Fill yourself up with high energy every day!

An affirmation that works for Michal is, "I am a superhero". She once saw a movie where one of the characters said this sentence to herself every time she did an important task. Michal uses it a lot because it really does give her strength and makes her feel like a superhero who can go about her daily tasks in the best way possible.

WATERING
YOUR ROOTS

Write down what strengths and powers you have that you can use to water your roots and help you grow.

Here's a list of words and phrases that can help you get going: brave, willpower, independent learner, team player, a good friend, strong, leader, initiator, reliable, confident, build people up, creative, you can count on me, responsible, funny, helpful, kind, happy, sporty, positive, curious—we're sure you can think of even more.

IT'S ALL IN
YOUR HEAD

What emotions do you experience in your daily life? Write about the different situations and feelings that come up. You can use these words to get you started: love, hate, disappointment, friendship, frustration, success, pride, sorrow, embarrassment, sadness, loneliness, pressure, confusion, shame, calm, enthusiasm, peace, surprise, excitement, strength, bravery, confidence, satisfaction.

THE RICE
EXPERIMENT

If you did the rice experiment yourself, tell us about it and your results. You can write, or draw pictures— be as creative as you want.

WHAT HAVE WE LEARNED?

IT'S ALL IN YOUR HEAD

Thoughts create your reality!

YOU HAVE THE ABILITY TO BE A HIGH ACHIEVER

Everyone can be a little better each day than they were yesterday!

NOURISH YOUR INNER WORLD TO DO WELL IN THE PHYSICAL WORLD

You have to make the effort to be better today if you want to be better.

HIGH ENERGY ALWAYS WINS

Do your goodnight ritual every night before going to sleep. Say a personal affirmation every day.

Code 5

Make Your Dreams Come True

"THE DAY a person **BORN** is they enter the STADIUM OF LIFE. THE DAY THEY understand why they were BORN THEY GO ONTO the field."

(Alon Ulman)

HOW TO CREATE THE FUTURE YOU WANT

We know you want to live a good life where you achieve all the things you dream about. The codes are your road to success and its secret is very simple: all you need to know is where you are today and where you want to go. What kind of life do you really want for yourself? Ask yourself, what movie do you really want to live in? This is exactly the Champion's Vision that we'll teach you to create and paint for yourself!

Champion's Vision: This is the image you have in your mind of your future. The best future you can imagine for yourself.

"Successful people have
a Champion's Vision.
They know what they want.
The rest know what
they don't want."
(Alon Ulman)

TO CREATE YOUR FUTURE, YOU SET GOALS!

O Most people regret the past, complain about the present and fear for the future.

O Champions learn from the past, live in the present and create their future.

O Your life is happening now and the best way to predict your future is to create it!

SET TARGETS!

WHEN? NOW!

In order to create your future, you need to know where you are now and where you want to go. That's basically the journey from the "You of Today" toward your "Greatest You". We're going to show you how to create your future by using the Champion's Codes to create your Champion's Vision!

Most people spend more time planning their birthday party or a trip than planning their entire lives.

Why does that happen? Because we're not taught how to plan our lives. In this code, we'll teach you how to change this.

Champions have plans for their lives, while other people wing it.
Remember the story *Alice's Adventures in Wonderland* by Lewis Carroll? If you haven't read the book, maybe you've seen one of the movies.

In the story, Alice is in Wonderland, and she finds herself at a crossroads where her path splits in two. Alice meets the Cheshire Cat and asks him which path she should take. The cat asks her where she wants to get to and Alice replies that she doesn't care. Then the cat tells her, if she doesn't care then it doesn't matter which path she chooses. Then Alice explains, she doesn't mind as long as she gets somewhere. Then the cat tells her she'll get somewhere if she walks long enough.

The message here is about **the importance of setting goals and targets**. If you don't have goals and targets for your life, and don't know where you want to go, or care what happens to you—then why should anyone else? People spend their free time on lots of things but rarely on planning for their future, when the biggest time waster is lack of direction.

There's a story about a study conducted a long time ago. We can't guarantee that it really happened, however its moral is clear and important. In this study, they took a group of students and asked them to answer questionnaires. After many years, they examined which students became successful people in their lives (judging by financial status, position and occupation, family, etc.). Then, they looked at the questionnaires answered when the participants were young. They wanted to see if it was already possible back then to know, according to their answers, who would be more successful in life. Out of all the questions, there was one question whose answer distinguished the students who became successful (about 10 percent of all students) and set them apart from all the others.

What do you THINK that QUESTION was?

It was: **Do you have goals in life?**

Those who became successful answered **yes** to this question.

Out of the successful students, those that became very successful answered yes to two more questions:

Are these GOALS WRITTEN?
and DO YOU LOOK at them EVERY DAY?

The majority of the students had answered no to each of these questions. A small amount had answered yes to the first question and had experienced some success in their lives. But the tiniest amount, who had achieved the most success had answered yes to all three questions.

In order to create the life you have always wanted in the future, you have today to consciously set yourself clear goals and targets.

In any case, you create your future by your own choices. However, just setting goals isn't enough—you need to make sure they're the kind of goals that will help you advance and grow.

This is why goals should be written and read every day.

This is exactly what **our method of creating your Champion's Vision** is based on:

- Have goals that will help you grow.

- Write them down.

- Read them every day.

Writing down goals will give you focus and, if you read them every day, you will significantly increase your chances of being a successful person and creating the life you want for yourself!

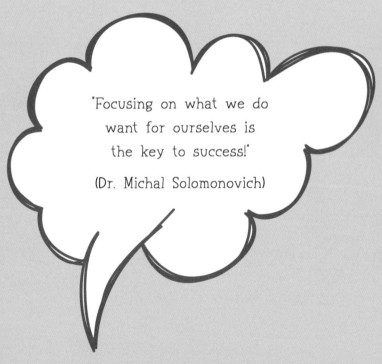

"Focusing on what we do want for ourselves is the key to success!"

(Dr. Michal Solomonovich)

EVERYTHING YOU FOCUS ON WILL GROW!

Everything you focus on, everything you put your efforts into, will grow! This is a cosmic law. Most people tend to focus on what they don't have, what they don't want—and that grows too. We want to teach you to focus on the positive things, on what you do want, so these things will grow.

THE ARROWS

Imagine a drawing of a person with arrows aimed toward their head, and then imagine a person with lots of arrows above their head and each one is pointing in a different direction.

What happens when there's focus and when there's none? What happens when your thoughts are focused and you don't let all the different ones in your head take you in different directions? Can you advance if the arrows aren't focused? It's easy to get distracted, so it's important to emphasize that we want you to be focused on exactly what you want!

Another STEP FORWARD

THE IMPORTANCE OF FOCUS

You may be familiar with an experiment involving the sun, a magnifying glass and a piece of paper. If you put the paper in front of the sun, nothing will happen to it. But if you take a magnifying glass and place it over the paper, the solar energy will cause the paper to heat up, and sometimes the paper will get hot enough for it to burn. This illustrates the importance of focus and power. We want you to do the same, because when you concentrate and focus on your goal it has great power, and your actions will achieve excellent results.

THERE ARE THREE TYPES OF GOALS

KNOWN GOALS

Goals that **you know you can achieve**, because you've achieved them in the past. For example, if you previously scored an A on your English test, you know it's possible to get an A on your next test as well.

NEW GOALS

Goals you haven't achieved yet, but **think you can achieve**. Maybe your friend with similar abilities has achieved something, so you think you can too. For example, your friend is on the basketball team, so you think you have a chance of joining the team too.

PEAK GOALS

Goals you can only dream of achieving right now. You want something but are not yet sure how to achieve it. This can be something that excites and terrifies you at the same time. Remember Daniel from *The Karate Kid*? He goes from being a beginner to winning the karate competition.

In your Champion's Vision, we ask you to think about all three of these types of goals. Don't just focus on the known goals because they feel easier or safer, but think about all the things you want to achieve, even if they sometimes feel out of reach.

So how do you do that? You have to use your imagination!

There's a well-known theory that our brain has two sides: the left side and the right. Although we don't know if the brain really does work like this, it is a great way of thinking about the two sides of ourselves and the way we work.

STRONG BRAIN

THE LEFT SIDE

The theory is that this side is your antenna, which receives information from the environment. It's responsible for logic, order and your practical side.

THE RIGHT SIDE

The theory is that this side is responsible for imagination, memory and your creative side.

Some people are more creative and seem more influenced by the right side of the brain, while others are more practical and seem more influenced by the left. Some people are able to thrive in both.

If you go to the gym and lift weights using only your right arm, your left arm will stay weak. And if you only use your left arm, your right will stay weak. If you train and lift weights with both arms, they'll both become strong.

The same thing could apply with the sides of yourself. You might be able to train your brain and become strong creatively and practically! **In order to create your Champion's Vision, we'd like to help you along the way because we want to train you to dream.**

The problem is we live in a world that overwhelms us with information from all directions, which can be stressful. Our way to relax and release pressure is to use our creative side in simple ways, like dancing, running, playing, listening to music and imagining.

Follow Your DREAMS

Everything starts off as a thought or an idea in someone's head and it only becomes reality if that person takes action. **In order to achieve your goals in life you have to imagine them first!**

HOW DO YOU CREATE A CHAMPION'S VISION?

You can do this anywhere but we recommend that you step outside, sit in the backyard, your favorite coffee shop—anywhere you feel comfortable and cozy.

NOW'S your time to THINK CREATIVELY and ask yourself THIS QUESTION:

In one year from now, what do you want to happen in your life? Most people work on lots of things but ignore the main project of their life. You're going to work on your main project—in all the different parts that make up your life: school, family, friends, hobbies, etc.

CREATIVE thinking

MY CHAMPION'S VISION

Name:...............................

Image:...............................

Goals:...............................

Think and ask yourself, a year from today:

- What would you like for yourself?

- What would you like to achieve?

- What kind of person do you want to be?

- Are there parts of your life (School, personal, social, family, hobbies, etc.) that need more focus?

Write your CHAMPION'S VISION in the PAST tense.

We're aiming for a year from today, so write the things you would like as if they've already happened. We know it sounds weird but this is part of the magic of the Champion's Vision.

The goal is to make you happy and excited about who you will become, and experience a little bit of the feeling you'll get when you reach the goals of your Champion's Vision. Your motivation for taking action every day will come from this feeling.

It feels AMAZING to be A REAL CHAMPION!

We also want you to add an image that will motivate you. You could include a picture of yourself where you're really happy: it could be a drawing or painting of you achieving your goal—anything you want. Adding this image is like adding a signature: it's your commitment that you will work to reach your Champion's Vision.

Remember — the way your Champion's Vision looks, could be the way your life looks a year from today.

GOODNIGHT RITUAL

Put your Champion's Vision by your bed: you can even hang it on the wall if you like.

Add this to the ritual we mentioned in Code 4 and, before going to sleep, take your Champion's Vision and read it aloud to yourself! Make sure you do it every night, seven days a week! It takes just a few seconds, but the impact is huge!

Remember, this is our "Wax on, Wax off", just like in *The Karate Kid*.

The effect this action will have on your subconscious, in those minutes before falling asleep, is tremendous. When you read the text written in the past tense you will feel, just for a moment, what it'll be like when you've already fulfilled your Champion's Vision. From here, the road to taking action and making your vision come to life feels possible!

Set yourself PEAK GOALS that excite and scare you at the same time, even if you don't think you can do them SUCCESSFULLY. This is HOW YOU START.

Your ritual now has two parts each night before going to bed: reading your Champion's Vision and the previous reading from Code 4 of the empowerment sentences.

QUESTION: What's the opposite of forgetting?

ANSWER: Remembering, obviously! (And writing is important because it'll help you remember and take action!)

YOUR THOUGHTS NOTEBOOK

We highly recommend that you always keep a small notebook with you throughout your day. This notebook joins the Lighthouse of the Month method (from Code 6). You can carry your notebook in your bag at school and keep it somewhere convenient for you at home.

The goal is to use your notebook to write down new ideas, thoughts, goals and targets. You can write down any actions that you're thinking of to advance your Champion's Vision. Of course, you can also write down activities, school projects, homework, chores and so on. Keep the notebook small enough so that it's easily accessible both at school and at home.

Don't forget to mark the tasks that you've already done.

YOU CAN IMPROVE ANYTHING IF YOU JUST FOCUS

Pick one thing to put more effort into this week and do it with maximum focus. Then write down what you chose to do and what your results were.

Remember: you have to plan in advance.

DREAM BIG AND MAKE BIG GOALS

Write about a peak goal you've thought about that excites you—it's okay if it scares you a little too.

THE TWO SIDES OF THE BRAIN

Circle the different strengths in the left and right sides of the brain that you think apply to you—you can add in extra ones you can think of too.

LEFT SIDE

Logic

Facts

Order

Practical

Rational

Good with numbers

RIGHT SIDE

Imagination

Visual

Brain storming

Creative

Artistic

Memory

WHAT HAVE WE LEARNED?

YOUR CHAMPION'S VISION

The image of the best future you can see and imagine for yourself a year ahead.

Everything you put effort into will grow.

THREE TYPES OF GOALS

• Known goals (current results).

• New goals (achievable goals).

• Peak goals (your dreams and aspirations).

Focusing on what you want to do is the key to success.

To achieve your Champion's Vision you have to set goals for your life, write them down and read them every day.

Use your thoughts notepad.

TWO SIDES OF THE BRAIN

We have different sides of ourselves—the left side (order, logic, practicality, etc.) and the right side (imagination, creativity, etc.).

Everything was once a thought or idea in someone's head that would never become a reality if that person hadn't taken actions.

GOOD NIGHT RITUAL

Your goodnight ritual—reading your Champion's Vision and the previous reading from Code 4 of the empowerment sentences.

GOOD NIGHT RITUAL

Code 6

Find Your Tribe

THE JOURNEY FROM THE "YOU OF TODAY" TO YOUR
"GREATEST YOU". SETTING GOALS AND TARGETS THAT
WILL ADVANCE YOU TOWARD YOUR CHAMPION'S VISION.

WHAT DOES THE WORD "TEAM" MEAN TO YOU?

Have you had the opportunity to be part of a team or find your "tribe"—that is, discover a group of people that you have a lot in common with? This could have been a sports team, a student council team at school, anything.

Think of the key elements that come to mind when you hear the word team. Here are some examples:

- O A strong connection between team members

- O Having clear direction toward success

- O Sharing a common goal

- O Teamwork and collaboration

- O Support and trust

People are selected and chosen to be on a team, which is one of the reasons everyone wants to be part of one. By reading this book, you're taking the steps so that you can make positive changes in your life and be a great member of any team.

You of Today   **Greatest You**

The smaller character represents the "You of Today" (this is where you are now) and the bigger character represents your "Greatest You" (this is where you want to be in the future, in all the different areas of your life). This refers to all the goals and targets you want to realize. This could be in the near future (in a few minutes, tomorrow, in a week) or in the more distant future (in a month, in three months, in a year).

YOU CAN GROW TOWARD YOUR "GREATEST YOU" BUT THERE ARE SOME PEOPLE WHO DON'T.

For example, today you might be able to score five free throws out of ten in a game. But, in three months, if you practice and put in the effort, you could be able to score nine free throws out of ten. If you get a low grade in the first semester, if you study and put in the effort, you can get a high grade in your second semester.

It's a **process of constant growth** where you work every day toward a "Greatest You". A "You" which is the best possible version of yourself!

We want to lead you toward your "Greatest You". We want to help you achieve individually and as part of a team, so that you're in a constant state of growth throughout your life and a little better every day than you were yesterday!

GROWTH and PROGRESS bring HAPPINESS!

We're not here to tell you that anything is possible, because that isn't completely true. You can't fly, or breathe underwater without oxygen, or time-travel, but one thing we know you can do is be a little better today than you were yesterday and every day after that! You can progress at any age and on your journey from the "You of Today" toward your "Greatest You" the only person you're competing with is yourself.

Another STEP FORWARD

In the 21st century, some of the professions we know today will become irrelevant. People will have to constantly evolve and develop new abilities, and it's a never-ending process, but this doesn't mean your process of growth can't also be fun, while also making you smarter and more successful. When you're constantly growing, you can become smarter, better friends to those around you, a better player in the team you're in, etc. This is what differentiates successful people from others. **If you're able to adapt and evolve throughout your entire life, you can be successful. You can take all the things you've learned into any field you choose!**

"In our champion's road to our goals, we explore the most interesting thing in the world - ourselves. In our research, we are both the researchers and the respondents."
(Dr. Michal Solomonovich)

Explore the most INTERESTING thing in THE WORLD!

Getting to know yourself and knowing more about yourself isn't just the most interesting thing, it's also the most important thing. There are a lot of people who don't really know themselves, or know how to take care of themselves. Your relationship with yourself is the most important relationship in the world because it's one that is irreplaceable.

We want you to get to know yourself better so you can work on the project that is most important: **your life!**

You'll learn more about yourself while reading this book and, hopefully, at every stage of your life.

SELF-DISCOVERY GOALS:

O Get to know yourself better.

O See what you're truly capable of.

O Find out what you want to achieve.

O Discover your strengths—you might even see new skills you never knew you had before.

O Look at your fears and what is stopping you and how to get past them.

O Learn how to motivate yourself and take action, not only when things are good for you but when they're difficult.

O Discover what makes you happy.

Let's ask you the most important question: why? Why do we want something? On the way to your "Greatest You" there will, of course, be problems, failures, fears and challenges. However, if you remember, the reason you want to achieve your goal, you can overcome any difficulty and this "why" will keep you strong all the way through any struggles you encounter.

Members of a team support each other, are happy for each other and want everyone to succeed. Your success should never come at the expense of someone else's success. You progress at your own pace without comparing yourself to anyone else, which means doing things for personal achievement and not for competition.

IF YOU'RE A PART OF A TEAM:

○ You're an example to others.

○ You can influence the results in your life.

○ You support other people.

○ You explore the most interesting thing in the world—yourself.

Ready? Let's get to work!!

"SUCCESS takes YEARS and along the way we mostly ENCOUNTER FRUSTRATIONS. CHAMPIONS are willing to pay the price to get what they want."

(Alon Ulman)

THE BIG THREE ON THE WAY TO YOUR CHAMPION'S VISION

Think of three big goals. These are peak goals: things that you thought you could only imagine or dream about: something that both excites you and scares you a little.

These are goals that you would like to set for yourself in the near future, usually for a period of six months up to a year. You can also use goals from your Champion's Vision.

The goals should be from three fields: school, personal and social—and they should be clearly worded so that you will know if you've achieved them.

In order to show you the level of detail required, we'll compare it to setting a destination on your phone in Google Maps. If you type in "New York City", the software won't take you to an exact location, because it's too wide a goal. But if you write "Rockefeller Centre, New York City", this is a clear and accurate goal, and Google will be able to take you exactly where you want to go. This is how your goals should be, worded in enough detail to get you where you need to be.

Write down your goal and your "why" below it. The "why" needs to answer three questions:

Answer these three questions:

○ Why is this goal important to me?

○ How will I feel when I achieve this goal?

○ How does this goal help me now and in the future?

Please note that the "why" should be yours and yours alone, not the "why" of your parents, teachers, friends, or anyone else. If the "why" isn't really yours, then any struggle that appears along the way, even the slightest, may cause you to give up the goal. If the "why" is yours, it means that the goal is important to you, and then a struggle, no matter how great, won't be able to distract you from your path in achieving it.

THE MONTHLY LIGHTHOUSE-NAVIGATING THE ROAD TO SUCCESS

So, you've set yourself goals —great! This is the first step.

What comes next?

How will we WORK TOWARD these GOALS?

This is the reason why for the **Monthly Lighthouse**. Do you know what a lighthouse is? It's a tall tower with a light that's placed near a beach. Ships use this as a beacon to navigate their way safely to shore.

The Monthly Lighthouse works similarly and is meant to help you navigate your way to success, and to your Champion's Vision. The lighthouse will direct you toward your Big Three goals. You'll be able to operate in the light of the lighthouse, just like the ships at sea. (*See the appendix at the end of this book.*)

The Big Three method and the Monthly Lighthouse are simple, practical methods that have, in recent years, helped lots of young people turn their goals and targets into plans of action and achieve them.

Each month we'll ask you to work on the Monthly Lighthouse and choose a small target that can be advanced that month, in order to reach your Big Three goals at the end of the process. Each target is written in the appropriate line (*see* the appendix). The first target in the lighthouse is related to school and the school goal in your Big Three; the second target is personal and is linked to the personal goal in your Big Three; and the third target is social and is connected to the social goal in your Big Three.

These TARGETS also need to be WRITTEN in detail, like we MENTIONED before.

Next, write down your name and what month you're in. Writing small targets alone isn't enough, we need you to write down your actions under each target—actions that you plan on doing for each of your targets in order to complete them successfully at the end of the month.

Actions should BE CLEAR, DETAILED AND PRACTICAL!

Don't write "I'll be a better student" or "I'll make more effort". These aren't actions but rather general statements. If your big goal is to eventually score 90 or higher in math, you can write in your monthly target, "Score an 80 in my next math test". Then write down exactly what you intend on doing in order to meet your small target. For example, "Every day at 4pm I'll do an extra 30 minutes on math homework". The Monthly

Lighthouse basically allows you to take small steps toward your big goal. Reaching this big goal is too difficult to achieve straight away, but taking a small step, with a small target each month toward your big goal, is much easier.

You can also use your notebook every day (*see* Code 5) to write down your actions, tasks, thoughts, goals, targets and more.

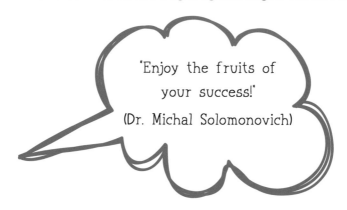

"Enjoy the fruits of your success!"
(Dr. Michal Solomonovich)

Your STAIRS to SUCCESS!

Each month use the Monthly Lighthouse as a step toward success in your bigger goals!

Reflect each month on your achievements.

So, after working hard all month and striving to fulfill your monthly target in each of the fields, the end of the month comes and:

PRACTICAL SUCCESS!
Have we mentioned that already?

At the end of each month, review your targets. Did you manage to meet them all? Observing the actions you've taken during the month is very important. (*See* the appendix at the end of the book.)

What have you ACHIEVED this MONTH?
DID YOU OPERATE IN THE LIGHT OF THE LIGHTHOUSE?

The very fact that you filled out the Monthly Lighthouse already means you've succeeded! Whether you've achieved the targets or not, the important thing is you've managed to learn something from it.

Ask yourself if you reached the targets you set for yourself. Whether you did or not, what did you learn from it? Even if the result wasn't what you wanted, it's okay, because you'll learn from this for next time.

If you were able to achieve your targets, ask yourself what were the actions that led you there. Keep following this path and more success will follow.

If you didn't achieve your targets, think about what you were able to learn. Examine your actions from a different perspective. Were they helpful? Think about what you can improve and what else you can do.

The "What I achieved this month" part is important and shows that if you take the same actions over and over again, you'll most likely get the same results over and over again. If you're happy with your results, that's great. But what if you're not? What if you're really not happy with your results and keep doing the same things over and over again—will that change anything? Probably not.

Similar actions will lead to similar results. Sometimes you'll need to change your actions and make a little more effort in order to achieve better results.

The lighthouse will keep you up to date on your progress and you'll be able to change course according to your development. There's no point in waiting six months, or a year, to find out if your actions are helping you. It's important to know this in real time, every month.

Your List of SUCCESSES— be PROUD OF YOURSELF.

How will you know if you've made progress? How can you maintain your successes? The answer is with a list.

Take a piece of paper and write the title:

"MY LIST OF SUCCESSES", followed by your name.

Your task, every day, for one entire month, is to write down all your successes—small, medium and large. Remember that overcoming a struggle is also a success. Write down at least two successes each day. (*See also* Code 2 for your list of successes and Compass of Success.)

It's IMPORTANT for you to constantly Look for YOUR SUCCESSES!

At first most kids think they have nothing to write, but slowly your successes will start to show up and the list will get longer every day. There's nothing like success to bring more success. You will see that when you work toward achieving your monthly targets and big goals, you will have many achievements!

You can list every success you think of: big successes, small successes, fun activities you participated in, spending time with your family or friends, a score on a test, playing well in a game— you could even list when you didn't hit one of your targets but were able to learn something important from that. The possibilities are endless.

"My List of Successes" will help you see your progress as well as maintain and bring more successes in the future. When your list is complete, just take another piece of paper and keep writing. The feeling you'll have when looking at your list will be a sense of pride. This is how champions feel, and when you make progress toward your "Greatest You" you'll feel that too.

Save your **Big Three goals** and **Monthly Lighthouse** alongside your list of **monthly achievements** and your **list of successes**. We suggest that you have a folder or notebook in which you can keep all your work. It's very important for you to be able to go back and look over all of your work so you can clearly see your progress in all the different areas of your life.

It's great fun seeing your own progress! We're very proud of you— and you should be too!

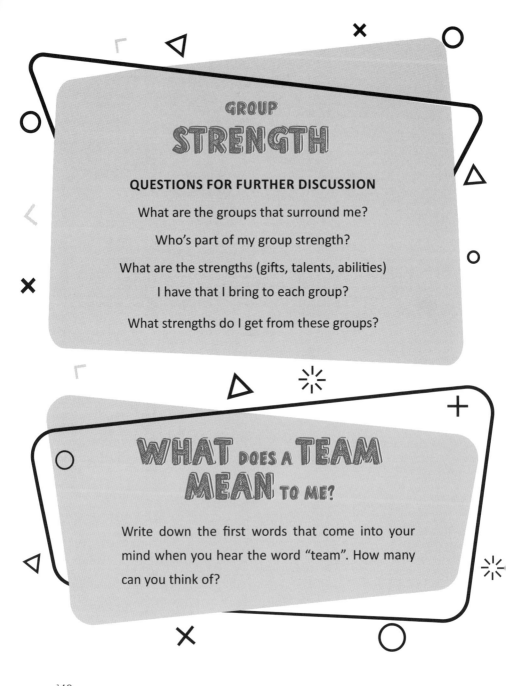

GROUP
STRENGTH

QUESTIONS FOR FURTHER DISCUSSION

What are the groups that surround me?

Who's part of my group strength?

What are the strengths (gifts, talents, abilities)
I have that I bring to each group?

What strengths do I get from these groups?

WHAT DOES A TEAM MEAN TO ME?

Write down the first words that come into your
mind when you hear the word "team". How many
can you think of?

WHAT HAVE WE LEARNED?

TEAM PLAYER

To be successful you need to be a team player.

"GREATEST YOU"

You're exploring the most interesting thing in the world—yourself. A journey from the 'You of Today' toward your 'Greatest You'!

You can be a little better today than you were yesterday.

LIFE IS YOUR PROJECT

Your main project is your life!

MY LIST OF SUCCESSES

Write down your successes, at least two a day.

THREE GOALS

Your Big Three goals will help you achieve your Champion's Vision. Three big goals in the fields of school, personal and social life.

MONTHLY LIGHTHOUSE

Small targets and actions for the upcoming month on the way to your big goals.

WHAT HAVE I ACHIEVED THIS MONTH?

Your self-reflection on the past month.

Code 7

Face Your Fears

Champions ask THEMSELVES A SPECIAL questioN: "WHY?"

Most people think and ask "**what**?". And then "**how**?"

What's your Champion's Vision? What is the best future you can imagine for yourself? What are the goals you would like to achieve for yourself?

How will the tools and methods help you get there?

Champions also ask these two questions, but they have a preliminary question.

CHAMPIONS ASK "WHY?"

It's your purpose; it gives you the motivation for action.

- Why? Purpose.
- What? Champion's Vision.
- How? Actions, tools.

CHAMPION'S VISION

"HE WHO HAS A WHY TO LIVE FOR CAN BEAR ALMOST ANY HOW."

This is a famous saying of Nietzsche, who was a philosopher.

The "why" is your destiny, the reason for your existence.

It's very important to know what the "why" is because a person who doesn't have a strong enough "why" will break on the first struggle they encounter (you can also refer to Code 6).

Once we know the "why", we can easily find the "what" to do (your Champion's Vision) and the "how" to do it (tools, actions, etc.).

"Heroes are not immune from fear, but people who act in spite of fear."

(Alon Ulman)

Finding the "WHY" is important for coping with DIFFICULTIES aLong THE WAY.

It's important that, from an early age, you find things to motivate you in life. Search for the "why" before taking action.

Think "WHY" you want to do WHAT you do in your LIFE.

Difficulties and fears will come and go. However, if you know your purpose, you'll know why your goal is important to you and it will be easier for you to overcome these problems.

DIFFICULTIES and OBSTACLES are inevitable in Life, but you can choose how YOU REACT TO THEM.

Everyone experiences difficulties but the difference in a champion is that they learn and grow from these problems and choose not to suffer from them. It's important to remember a champion knows they're the director of their life because they're in control and responsible. A champion doesn't blame anyone for their problems, so they work harder, learn from the things that happened to them and create a better future for themselves.

Paul Stoltz is an expert who writes about perseverance and has developed a method in helping people to overcome difficulties. Erik Weihenmayer went blind when he was young, due to illness, and then began climbing mountains, becoming one of the most successful blind athletes of all time. He was the first blind man to reach the summit of Mount Everest and has since climbed all seven of the highest peaks in the world. In their joint book, *The Adversity Advantage: Turning Everyday Struggles into Everyday Greatness*, they both talk about how to overcome difficulties and have a meaningful life.

Erik Weihenmayer had every reason to give up but, in spite of that, his choice was to find something that he was good at and pursue it. The choice was entirely in his hands.

LET'S CLIMB A MOUNTAIN!

There are three types of behavior among mountain climbers: settlers, parkers and climbers.

Settlers: They don't even start climbing and just tell themselves they can't do it and settle at the bottom of the mountain.

Parkers: They started climbing, set up a camp and stayed there to rest. They know the situation isn't exactly what they wanted, but they don't take action to change it. Parking is a natural thing—to reach where we want and park. This also depends on how long you stay in parking. If you stay in parking for too long, it becomes a negative thing. People who have parked will look at the summit and think they have no reason to continue, that the place they've reached is good enough, so they'll just stay there.

Climbers: These are the champions. People with a different way of thinking, who advance toward the top, in spite of all the difficulties and obstacles along the way. They try again and again, as many times as it takes until they reach the top.

Depending on the area of their lives, different people choose different courses of action; some settle, some park and some climb.

Think about a challenging class at school. The settlers are the ones that say, "I'm no good at this", and think no matter what they do they can't win. They simply give up. The parkers will climb a bit, reach an okay grade and tell themselves they don't have the skills to reach higher, so it's not worth the effort. The climbers are the ones who won't give up and will continue over and over again. They will practice a bit harder, invest more time in studying, ask for help, learn from their mistakes and will never give up until they reach their goal.

It's important to remember that one of these terms won't apply to you in every aspect of your life. For example, you can be a settler in sports, a parker in your science class at school and a climber in your social life.

Questions for SELF-REFLECTION

Where are you in different areas of your life? Think about your different classes at school, your social life, family life and any sports or hobbies you spend time doing. In which areas are you climbing and achieving?

Be honest with yourself and write down where you feel like you're giving up, where you feel like you're parking and would like to switch to climbing. What difficulties are you facing? What and who can help you overcome these so you can start climbing?

CLIMB YOUR EVEREST!

LET'S BREAK THE BOUNDARIES OF FEAR!

We can teach you a great way to do it!

Peak goals: **what you really want.**

New goals: **what you think you can do.**

Known goals: **what you've already done.**

Fear reaches us on the border between known/new goals and peak goals.

Known goals are the ones you've already achieved and new goals are things you think you can achieve (*see also* Code 5). In these two types of goals, you're not afraid because you've already achieved them or think they're possible. Peak goals, are a different story because fear can take over before you accomplish your dream.

Everyone is scared, but champions take action and advance despite their fear, while others remain paralyzed and stay put. We'd like to teach you a clear and focused method on how to overcome the fear barrier and break your own boundaries. Champions don't see non-action as an option and that's why they succeed. Our method will help you with that concept. Are you ready?

THE SIX STAGE FORMULA TO BREAKING BOUNDARIES:

1. **Goal:** Choose a goal that you feel strongly about achieving—a peak goal, something thrilling, exciting and even scary. A goal you really want.

2. **A mental breakthrough:** The understanding that you're capable of achieving it. And remember your "Why". Why is this goal important to you? Why do you want to achieve it? Answering these questions will help you overcome all the difficulties along the path.

3. **First step toward your goal:** Actually taking action. Even if it's a small step, take it. For example, if you want to start working out and running, the first step could be getting running shoes.

4. **Build a continuous plan of action** toward that goal. A sequence of actions that will bring you toward your goal. Think about what we said about progress and use the Monthly Lighthouse, "What have I achieved this month?", and "My List of Successes" to help you along the way. Work using the stairs of success, with small targets and steps each month to get to your big goal.

5. **Act like a torpedo:** A torpedo is an underwater weapon used against other sea vessels. As soon as it is shot, it's focused on its goal and nothing can stop it from hitting it. That's the way you need to be. The minute you've made up your mind that you're going for it, no matter what others say. No matter how many people try to bring you down and tell you that you can't do it, or that you're not good enough. Your brain is shut to negative influences.

6. **Create a supportive environment that will encourage you to continue:** Surround yourself with people who are true friends, who will support and assist you in reaching your goals.

If you invest 90 minutes a day for 10 years—you can be a champion in anything you choose!

We highly recommend that you combine the Six Stage Formula to Breaking Boundaries with the 10,000 rule (*see* Code 3).

Be a torpedo—10,000 times, if necessary—to achieve your goal! People who want to achieve their goals need to "pay the price". Investing even 10,000 hours or 10,000 attempts, because you cannot succeed without paying the price.

Questions for SELF-REFLECTION

FINDING YOUR FEAR BARRIER

Please think about and answer the following questions:

- O What are the things that scare you?

- O What scares you the most?

- O Why does this scare you?

- O What's scary about it?

- O What are the things that stop you from reaching your goals?

- O What are you struggling with?

If there was no chance of you failing, what's the next step you would take toward your target?

What will happen to you when you achieve your goal and how will you feel?

You can stop being SCARED the day you realize that you can make all YOUR FEARS come TRUE.

Remember, what we said earlier, that thought creates reality. So, if you expect to be scared you will be. We call this a self-fulfilling prophecy (see Code 4).

Real FEAR versus IMAGINARY fear

There is a legend about a grandfather who told his grandson a bedtime story:

Every human being has a good wolf and a bad wolf. The good wolf symbolizes the kindness, gentleness, honesty, love and other positive qualities that exist in each person. The evil wolf symbolizes the fear, anger, selfishness and other negative qualities that also exist. The grandfather tells the grandson that every day the wolves fight amongst themselves within each human. Then, the grandson asks: "Grandpa, which wolf wins?" And the grandfather answers: "The wolf that you feed more."

The moral of the story is that we are the directors of our lives and only we can decide whether we let fear take over or overcome it!

There are two types of fear: real fear and imaginary fear. How they make you feel is really similar, but it's very important that you know the difference between them. Seeing what is real fear, versus what is imaginary fear, is a great way to overcome this feeling.

IMAGINARY FEAR

Imaginary fear is created as a result of a thought that something bad might happen. However, the thing has not yet happened and only exists in our imagination. The physical reaction in your body is real. However, fear is imaginary and it's created by thought. For example, a kid who's afraid of monsters at night. You know there's nothing for the kid to be scared of, but that doesn't make it any less real for them.

REAL FEAR

Real fear is a state of real danger that occurs in reality. For example, a snake that's crawling next to you and could bite, or a car that's going very fast and might hit you.

We'll give you an example where the situation described is similar but the fear is different—one's imaginary and the other's real.

In the first case, a man is scared of flying. He's sitting on a plane and throughout the entire flight, he fears the plane will crash. He feels scared even though everything's fine on board, there's no warning from the cockpit about any problem and the plane lands safely. Isn't it a waste for him to sit through the entire flight worried? Of course, this person's fear of flying is an imaginary fear. The plane and passengers weren't in danger, and the man had no real reason to be afraid.

In the second case, during a flight, the pilot announces a major problem with the plane and that the plane is about to crash. The man experiences real fear because his life and the other passengers' lives are in real danger. Only in a situation like this where there is real danger, does the fear of flying become a real fear.

Try to think how many times in your life you have come across real fear. Very few. Real fear is a plane crash, a wild animal walking freely along the street, a terrible car accident, etc. In those cases, lives are in actual danger, but these are rare.

- Most of the fears you experience are imaginary fears, not real ones.

- Courage can be developed. You can take action despite fear!

- Your target is to break the fear barrier.

- How do you do that? Using your thoughts, with the help of your Compass of Success!

Every time you feel even just a little bit of fear, ask yourself if the fear you're starting to feel is a real fear. Are you truly in real danger? Or is it just the thought of something that might happen?

If the answer is no, throw those thoughts out of your head and tell yourself that it's just an imaginary fear, so it isn't worth thinking about!

Ask yourself, "Does it advance me to be afraid of something that's just an imaginary fear? Will it help me achieve what I want?". Obviously not: imaginary fear won't advance you, it'll only make you achieve less in life.

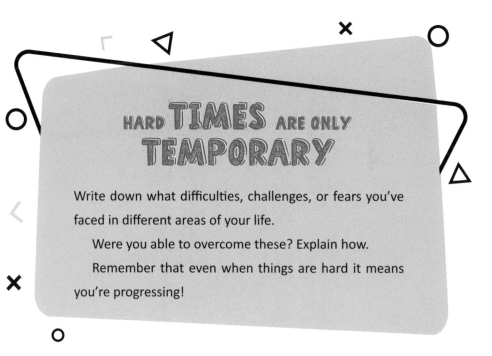

HARD TIMES ARE ONLY TEMPORARY

Write down what difficulties, challenges, or fears you've faced in different areas of your life.

Were you able to overcome these? Explain how.

Remember that even when things are hard it means you're progressing!

LET'S CLIMB A
MOUNTAIN

Write in each of the areas of your life where you're climbing on your personal Everest.

Where have you settled? Where have you parked? Where have you climbed? It's not too late to change.

Look at each of your subjects here.

School   **settled/parked/climb**

Personal   **settled/parked/climb**

Social   **settled/parked/climb**

Family   **settled/parked/climb**

Hobbies/Sports   **settled/parked/climb**

WHAT HAVE WE LEARNED?

CHAMPION'S FEEL FEAR

Heroes still feel afraid but take action despite the fear.

CHAMPIONS ASK "WHY?"

Champions ask "Why?" and only then do they ask "What?" and "How?"

"He who has a why to live for can bear almost any how."

In the past, have you been a settler, parker or climber?

There will always be difficulties but suffering is a choice.

Real fear versus imaginary fear.

THE SIX STEP FORMULA FOR BREAKING BOUNDARIES.

Breaking the fear barrier using rational thought and your Compass of Success

Courage can be developed.

Code 8

Anything You Want to Get, Give!

"DO something for OTHERS with no intention OF GETTING ANYTHING BACK FROM THEM. Your return is already coming."

(Dr. Michal Solomonovich)

ANYTHING YOU WANT TO GET, GIVE!

This is a super-principle for champions.

What does SUPER-PRINCIPLE mean?

We mean something that is very, very, very, very important!

This is a principle that affects all the codes in the book and is the way to build good relationships with family, friends and acquaintances—and in the future, when you grow up, a way to succeed in business.

This isn't a deal. You don't give something to someone to get something back. This means **doing something for someone else, without having any intention of getting something in return**. To give—not in order to receive—only for the sake of giving.

Has anyone ever told you that if you want to be treated with respect you have to treat others with respect? This is a similar value and positive way of thinking that we hope will stay with you throughout your life.

If you WANT LOVE, you have to GIVE LOVE.

If you want to be happy, you have to make others happy. If you want to participate in a game, you have to invite others to participate in the game. **Your life is a reflection of what you do — like a mirror.**

YOUR
LIFE IS A
REFLECTION
OF WHAT
YOU DO

Giving VALUE to OTHERS.

THE LAW OF CAUSE AND EFFECT is a law that says every result is preceded by a reason. So, when you are treated a certain way, there is always a reason behind it, even if it isn't to do with you directly. However, by giving to others, you create a positive future. People don't always understand the law of cause and effect when it comes to relationships, because of the dimension of time.

Think about what would happen if you put your hand over a burning fire. You would immediately pull your hand away because you feel the heat right away. You can figure out what the outcome would've been if you had kept your hand over the fire. The result (the feeling of heat) comes immediately after the cause (leaving your hand over the fire). So, in this situation, the law of cause and effect is clear. When it comes to relationships with people, the time between cause and effect can be longer. You could do something bad, or start behaving rudely, but you might not see the result—in the way others start to treat you—for a long time. It's more difficult to understand the law of cause and effect in this way because more time passes between the cause and the effect. This doesn't stop this law being true and important in every area of your life.

EVERYTHING in the WORLd has A CAUSE and an EFFECT.

People who help others in life achieve more in their own lives. When you start giving and helping out, you'll find that the universe has a way of bringing that kind of positive behavior back to you.

THE BOY AND THE BIKE SALE

A boy sees an old bike lying by his neighbor's house. He asks the neighbor if he can buy the bicycle for $11. The neighbor is happy to sell the bike because he wants to get it out of his yard. The boy repairs the bike, paints it, straightens the handlebars, inflates the wheels and now the bike looks much better. The boy hears that another neighbor is looking to buy a bicycle as a gift for his son's birthday. The boy offers the bike to the other neighbor for $15. The neighbor buys the bike and everyone is happy. The first neighbor got the old bicycle out of his yard, the second neighbor got a gift for his son at a really good price, the birthday boy got a new bike and the boy who repaired the bicycle earned money.

If the boy had done a bad job fixing up the bike, he wouldn't have made any money. The boy got the money for the value he created. He turned the old rusty bike into a great bike, helped one neighbor clear trash, helped another neighbor make his son happy and helped himself because he made some money!

THE KING AND HIS TWO ASSISTANTS

Assistant one earned three golden coins per month and assistant two earned ten golden coins. Assistant one was unhappy that assistant two was earning more than him for the same amount of work. Assistant one asks the king for a raise and the king tells him he'll think about it.

At the same time, a huge convoy arrives in the city. The king calls assistant one and asks him to find out more about it. Assistant one goes and comes back, and tells the king that there are 500 people in the convoy. The king asks him where the people have come from. The assistant goes to ask, comes back and tells him they came from the next city. The king asks the assistant the purpose of their visit. The assistant goes to ask, comes back and tells him that they've come to work in the city. The king asks where the people will be living. The assistant goes to ask, comes back and tells him the street they'll be living on. The king asks if they'd like to meet with him. The assistant goes to ask, comes back and tells him they'd love to meet him. The king asks, "When would they'd like to come?" The assistant goes to ask, comes back and tells him they'll come tomorrow morning.

At this point, the king asks assistant one to sit beside him as he calls assistant two. The king gives assistant two the same order he originally gave to assistant one, to find out about the convoy. Assistant two goes to ask, comes back and tells the king there is a convoy of 500 people, they came from the next city to find work. He also tells the king the street they'll be living on and that they'd love to meet the king tomorrow morning. The king then turns to assistant one and says to him, "Now you realize why assistant two gets ten coins while you only get three!".

Both assistants had the same job but their value to the king was not the same, so their payment was not the same. Assistant two made one trip and found out all the information needed, so the king didn't need to ask him additional questions. In comparison, assistant one didn't find out all the information by himself and needed to get new instructions from the king each time. His work took more time and he needed to be guided at every step, so the value of his work was lower.

Give FIRST — and ONLY then RECEIVE!

True giving is given from the heart where nothing is expected in return. We want you to adopt a general attitude of giving in life, where you do things for others because it makes you feel good to give and help friends. If you only give because you expect something in return, you're making a deal instead of acting out of true kindness and shouldn't be surprised when you don't get the results you want.

This principle is significant and affects every area of your life. You can start with simple things, like calling a sick friend and asking how they're doing, helping a friend catch up on the class they missed, explaining something to a friend who's struggling to understand their homework, and so on.

We've all had a Secret Santa gift we've been disappointed in, right? Imagine if everyone gave their gift according to the super-principle of anythinig you want to get, give. Everyone would come home happy because everyone would have brought a gift they'd be happy to receive—and that creates true giving from the heart.

You are WHAT YOU DO!

IF YOU DO GOOD THINGS AND GIVE VALUE TO OTHERS, YOU ENCOURAGE GOOD THINGS TO HAPPEN TO YOU.

On the other hand, if you do negative things, people might start to treat you in a negative way.

This is how giving works. If you give and help because you want everyone to succeed and not for the purpose of getting something in return, others will do the same for you too.

It always WORKS out in THE END.

YOUR GOOD DEED WON'T ALWAYS COME BACK TO YOU IMMEDIATELY—IT CAN TAKE TIME, sometimes even years. It won't always come back to you from the same person, but if you're persistent and act according to this principle, your good deeds will always come back to you!

We've done a lot of things in our lives without knowing how they would affect us in the future. Today, we realize that all the time and skills we've invested are the things that have made us who we are today.

Our ACTIONS and INVESTMENTS come back to us.

IT'S VERY IMPORTANT TO INVEST IN YOUR SKILLS AND YOURSELF.

It will always come back to you in the future. If you invest in yourself (for example, study hard in school), you'll reap the rewards along the way and be able to enjoy them!

Invest in yourself so that everything you give to the world has value.

Is what I am GIVING having an IMPACT on what I RECEIVE?

Let's understand the super-principle from another angle. Although we can't control how people treat us or the things that happen to us, it is useful to think about how our behavior might be influencing what we get. If you were to give other people what you'd like to receive, according to the super-principle, you'd eventually get it back. So if you're not getting this it's time to examine what you're putting out into the universe. For example, if you're not picked for a soccer game, instead of getting upset and arguing about it, you can stop for a moment and ask yourself, "Will this advance me?". Instead of getting angry, reflect honestly on how you've been acting and what impact this might have had on this result.

Did you REALLY give what you WANTED to RECEIVE?

Did you really give for the sake of giving and not just to get something in return? If you practiced and always thought about how to be a good team player in the game, then they probably would have picked you to play, right?

Take, for example, a person at a workplace who isn't happy with their salary. Think about what will happen if that person makes a change, contributes to the business and comes to work fully motivated. The value they give to the workplace will increase and they'll eventually get a raise, or use this positive change to get an even better job. The same theory applies in school, with your friends, family and so on.

If you adopt this way of thinking, you'll be able to achieve the things you really want for yourself. You can make small changes in your behavior toward others and, in the chain reaction that follows, the way others treat you will also change and you'll be much happier with your results.

You NEED to put IN THE WORK.

It won't be easy right from the start. Think of it as a weight training workout in a gym. At first it's really hard, but the more you train, the easier it'll be to lift those weights. The exact same thing happens here. The more positive changes you put out into the universe, the more it will become second nature, the better your results will be and the happier you'll be with the way other people treat you.

ALways SEEK to make others FEEL GOOD.

Think about warm colors: yellow, orange, purple, pink, etc.—they create feelings of happiness, joy and positivity.

Then think about gloomy black-and-gray colors—do they make you feel differently?

Think about a fight you've had with someone lately. If they insulted you and hurt you emotionally, after a short time you won't be able to remember word for word what they told you, but you won't be able to forget how they made you feel.

Your goal is to **make every person you meet feel good**, like the warm colors. So the person you have finished talking to will remember that you left them happy and positive, and that feeling will come straight back to you from them.

It's important to remember that **the things you do for others can stay with them forever**!

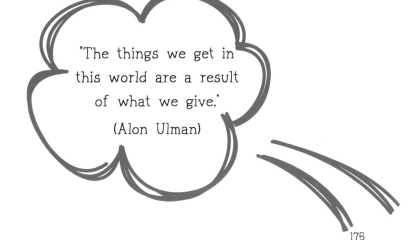

"The things we get in this world are a result of what we give."
(Alon Ulman)

If you try to bring VALUE to others, you'll achieve BETTER RESULTS and HAPPINESS for yourself.

The more you act according to the super-principle of "Anything you want to get, give", the more you'll get back from the world.

As we explained earlier, those good things can take time and won't necessarily come back to us from the same person we gave to. But one thing's for sure—**doing good will help you**. You'll feel better about yourself, for helping others and giving what you would be happy to receive!

HAPPINESS = GIVING; GIVING = HAPPINESS.

Doing good deeds causes others to return with good feelings, appreciation, love and joy—and **this is how we create a better world**.

We want you to take a large piece of paper or cardboard and create a sign for your room that says "Anything you want to get, give". Hang it by your bed, above your desk or on your door. This way you can look at this sign every day and it'll remind you to follow it.

Another STEP FORWARD

DIRECT GIVING VERSUS INDIRECT GIVING

The super-principle can be put into action through direct giving as well as indirect giving. **Direct giving** is your direct action that affects other people. **Indirect giving** is created when you act directly, and the person influenced by your action continues to act according to the principle and influences other people. Imagine a chain of good deeds, where each person in the chain acts according to the principle, causing the next person to act in this way too.

It makes us feel great to see that we've influenced and helped not only one person, but that our circle of influence is constantly expanding.

ANYTHING YOU WANT TO GET, GIVE!

Write about situations where you've applied this super-principle in your life. Then write down where you think you can apply this in the future.

Then, write about an area in your life where you plan to act on this in the future. What will you do? What do you think will happen?

WHAT HAVE WE LEARNED?

THE SUPER-PRINCIPLE

"Anything you want to get, give."

First you give and only then do you receive!

THE LAW OF CAUSE AND EFFECT

When you make an effort to help others, you'll achieve better results.

THE EXTENDED SUPER-PRINCIPLE

If you're unhappy with what you're getting from others, look at what you're giving to others.

DOING GOOD DEEDS WILL HELP YOU PROGRESS IN LIFE.

A good deed will always come back to you even if it takes a long time and is not necessarily from the same person you helped.

A chain of good deeds can create a better world.

Code 9

Live Your Best Life

CHAMPIONS CREATE AN ENVIRONMENT FOR THEMSELVES THAT BRINGS THEM TOWARD THEIR GOALS!

An environment *is* STRONGER than WILLPOWER

To be a champion you must create an environment that will bring you closer to your goals. This environment is both internal and external. In this code we'll mainly talk about the external environment.

INTERNAL ENVIRONMENT: Your thoughts, your feelings, your values, your internal stories, the actions you choose and so on. You control the internal environment. All of the codes in this book are designed to help you advance your internal environment for yourself, toward the internal Champion's environment!

EXTERNAL ENVIRONMENT: The people and circumstances that surround you. These are the people you spend your daily life with, such as friends and family. The kids you hang out with at school or after school, in your sports team or dance practice, and even the kids you play computer games with or the Internet, or the friends you have on social media.

While the external environment depends on the other people around you, you can also control it and choose the people who surround you. The friends you hang out with are your choice.

A person can CHANGE their ENVIRONMENT.

You need to create an environment that will help you. There are environments that can be created and changed, like friends, and there are environments that you are given, like family.

The largest trees in the world are redwoods (giant sequoia), and the smallest trees in the world are bonsai trees, miniature trees that grow as high as 30–40 cm.

Bonsai trees are so small because they're not allowed to grow. This is a delicate Japanese art. The roots of the trees are tied, their branches are pruned over time with patience and the end result is a very beautiful tree. They can't really grow, but (and this is important) **they have the potential to grow and it's external factors that prevent them from doing that.**

Sequoia trees, on the other hand, are huge. Some of them are so big that if you search them online, you'll find pictures where you see huge circles of people surrounding one redwood tree.

Does a bonsai tree have the ability it needs to be bigger? The answer is yes.

Some people act as if their roots are tied but you can choose to be a redwood or a bonsai tree. The lesson here is simple: unlike a tree, a person can choose. **Even if someone tries to tie your roots, you can resist and grow.**

Can your FRIENDS HELP create your Champion's ENVIRONMENT?

WHICH FRIENDS DO YOU THINK WOULD BE BEST FOR THIS?

Do you surround yourself with friends who can help you? Those who bring out the best in you? Or the ones who bring you down?

Of course, this choice is personal.

You might be familiar with the saying "Tell me who your friends are and I will tell you who you are." This is a very true statement. Your behavior, your aspirations, your results, are greatly influenced by your environment.

If you feel that your environment is supportive and helpful, that's great. But what if it's not? What if you feel, even though it might be a little hard to admit, that your friends aren't the best for your Champion's environment?

Here are some warning signs to look out for if you're worried about your friends:

○ They're not happy for you.

○ They're jealous of you.

○ Everything always centers around them.

○ You often feel uncomfortable around them.

○ You often get angry and upset around them.

○ They bring you down.

○ They behave aggressively toward you.

○ They're dishonest or unreliable.

○ They often get you to do things you don't like and don't feel good about doing.

○ They keep you away from your goals and drain your energy.

In cases like this you have to ask, how can I change this environment?

It's important to be AWARE of your ENVIRONMENT and those IN IT!

An environment can be changed. Just being aware of the environment you're in and thinking about ways to improve it is already progress.

You don't have to have friends around you that are unhelpful and unsupportive.

Signs that your friends help create a Champion's environment:

○ They give you energy.

○ They have goals and targets in their lives.

○ You can collaborate with them.

○ They share some of your goals and values.

○ They're happy for you when you succeed.

○ You can share your successes with them.

○ They help you when you need it.

Your environment ISN'T FIXED —you can CHANGE IT!

CREATE A SUPPORTIVE ENVIRONMENT AROUND YOU WITH OTHER CHAMPIONS—PEOPLE WHO HELP YOU TO BE YOUR GREATEST YOU!

The key to change is to surround yourself with people you want to resemble more, or who challenge your abilities.

Alon remembers what it was like when he started training for the Iron Man competition, which is a really difficult sporting race. He joined an environment of people with very high physical abilities and wanted to be like them. When he started training, at first it was incredibly hard to keep up, but he stayed with them and because of that was able to reach a much higher level of fitness. He surrounded himself with champions and became one too!

Is an ENVIRONMENT stronger than WILLPOWER?

You already know that in order to reach your goals, you need to be consistent. Willpower is also important because it's the thing that motivates you to take action, to achieve the things you want for yourself. For example, willpower is the thing that stops you talking in class and interrupting—even though you'd prefer to talk to your friends—because you understand that it's important to listen in class to pass.

It's not always easy to exercise willpower.

When you're in a Champion's environment, the friends that surround you can help, even when your willpower weakens and you're almost ready to give up.

Unsupportive friends will never be happy for you when you succeed. They'll try to bring you down and point out your weaknesses.

On the other hand, **supportive friends** will always be happy for you when you do well. Most importantly, they'll encourage you and push you forward in times of need. When you create a Champion's environment of supportive people, these are the friends that won't give up on you, even when you're willing to give up on yourself.

Your Champion's environment is often stronger than willpower and it can help you in difficult moments. Think of a sports competition. Even when the team loses, the fans, the coach and the team members don't give up—they continue to encourage and strengthen the players, even in the most difficult moments.

Think about school. If you're in a difficult class, you have to commit to studying harder and putting in more effort. Even though this can be tough, you're investing in your future success.

Your CHAMPION'S environment creates POWER.

In cycling competitions, there is a riding structure called peloton, from the French word meaning platoon, because the riders progress in the group like a military unit.

But why do they ride like this? This arrow-shaped structure helps them reduce the resistance of the air. The power of the group in the arrow structure reduces the cyclists' effort. Riders in the front of the arrow absorb air resistance and those in the middle are protected which makes the riding easier for them. They take turns moving to the outside of the arrow structure, so everyone gets time to rest and enjoy an easier ride. Riding in this structure increases the chances of success. Migrating birds also fly in an arrow-shaped structure for the same reason.

The birds and the cyclists in the peloton are both examples of **supportive environments**.

Surround yourself with people who will be there for you and support you so that you can achieve success!

A CHAMPION'S ENVIRONMENT CREATES ANOTHER POWER: THE POWER OF THE GROUP. WHEN YOU ADD THIS TO THE PERSONAL POWER THAT EXISTS WITHIN YOU, YOU'LL BE UNSTOPPABLE.

Look at the following simple math exercise: $1 + 1 = 2$.

To explain to you the power of the Champion's environment, another way to solve this exercise is as follows: $1 + 1 > 2$.

We, of course, understand that mathematically this is incorrect, but in the Champion's environment, it is very true.

You have an individual power (1). But if you unite forces it can lead to greater results than you could ever get individually!

This is the great thing about teamwork and the Champion's environment! That is what makes $1 + 1$ greater than 2.

Uniting different forces, when you have a common goal, creates the greatest power.

Think of a basketball team. Each player is talented, but when they play as a unified and strong team, the power of the team is greater and worth more than the talent of the individuals. If you took five players, even the best players in the world, and placed them all as point guards, the team probably wouldn't be very successful because there are other positions that need to be filled in order for them to function at their best. Each of these roles is important because it's how they work together that creates the strength of the group.

Learn from the BEST and copy SUCCESSES!

A Champion's environment allows you to do another thing, which is very important—copying success. Not in a negative sense, like copying a test, but **learning from the best** and copying their successes. You see a kid who's very successful in something, in a sport, a test, a class— ask them how they did it. It's better to apply things that have already worked than to reinvent the wheel. The best shortcut in the world is learning from someone who's already been there and managed to do something similar.

You probably know kids in class who always get good grades on their tests. Instead of assuming they're just lucky, you should think about why this happens. The chances are they're not just winging it.

They're DOING something DIFFERENT.

If you want to achieve good results like those kids, you should ask yourself: what are they doing differently?

It's smart to LEARN from the BEST, copy their SUCCESS and shorten the way to your OWN SUCCESS.

It's not complicated, sometimes it's just a simple question. You can ask a friend, or person in your class who's good at something you want to be good at too. This method is often easier than starting from scratch yourself.

It's better to find a shortcut, learn from the best and do the same thing they're doing. Behind every high-achieving person or friend, there's a success story about how they got there. You can learn from them and apply their methods to your life as well.

Of course, you can use this method in other areas, not just in school. If you want to be able to play basketball better, look at what professional players do and learn from them. If you want to be chosen for the main part in a dance show, you can look at what a good dancer does, what their training methods are and learn from them. Most people will be happy to share their knowledge with you and help you achieve success. You've already learned:

CHAMPIONS are HAPPY for others and COMPLIMENT THEM!

ANOTHER STEP FORWARD

1 + 1 > 2 is actually a synergy!

Synergy is the joint action of two or more entities, which allows for a better result together than separately.

It works the same way in business. Partners complement each other when they each have different strengths, but have a common dream to succeed in business.

The sum 1 + 1 = 0 can also be true. Not mathematically, but in life. When there's no cooperation between people, no teamwork and people are fighting with each other, the power of each of them is weakened because they don't have a Champion's environment.

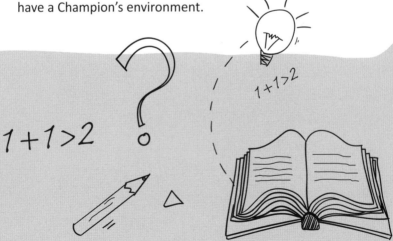

The key to CHANGE is being around PEOPLE you want to BE LIKE.

MASTER MINDS

In simpler words, talk to people who are part of your Champion's environment. Successful **adults always have a group of people they consult with**, like a forum. It exists in politics, in business and basically every field. Just like in Code 6, we recommend that you talk, ask for advice and help from other people, like friends, family, teachers and coaches, etc.

There's no point in asking people you already know won't support you or offer encouragement. You could have a weekly talk with a friend where you share your goals and targets, give each other advice and make plans that will help you move forward. You can also do this in a group and whenever someone needs advice on a particular topic, you can get together and talk about it. You can talk to your family, your parents, siblings or even a teacher you feel comfortable with. Each person brings their own expertise and their own knowledge in different ways. Think of it as **a group of experts** with whom you can consult whenever you need.

A Champion's ENVIRONMENT challenges your abilities and MAKES you the BEST version of YOURSELF.

MAKE DECISIONS QUICKLY AND CHANGE YOUR MIND SLOWLY

Successful people make decisions fast, even if they're not 100 percent sure, and change their mind slowly. There will be times when you'll have to make decisions when you're unsure. If you wait too long without making a decision, you've basically decided that the answer is no. Making a decision, no matter what it is, even if in the end it turns out to be wrong, is better than doing nothing out of fear.

Changing your mind slowly is important because this will keep you on track when you're faced with difficulties and challenges along the way. It takes more than one action and often a lot of work to achieve a goal, if you're determined this will keep you going toward your target.

Some people struggle to move forward because they hesitate in making decisions, they keep changing their minds all the time. When you're in a Champion's environment, **you can make decisions easily and faster** because you have a group of successful people to learn from and guide you.

To know if you're in a Champion's environment, you need to ask: Who are the people surrounding you? What are they doing for you? How do they make you think? What kind of person do they make you want to be? Are you okay with that?

It's impossible to SWIM Like a SHARK when you're hanging out with SARDINES.

This sentence precisely explains the importance of your Champion's environment! If you want to swim like a shark and live like a shark, then you can't hang out with sardines. A small fish will never be able to swim like a shark. We want you to live in a Champion's environment that matches your aspirations and your goals. This will make you raise your standards and behavior in all areas, because it's easier to succeed in a supportive environment.

What is the SOCIAL LAW of AVERAGES?

The social law of averages states that **a person will be the average of the five people they spend the most time with**.

If you want to reach your "Greatest You", you need to surround yourself with champions. You want an environment where the average is high—think about the five people you spend the most time with. Do you want those people to influence who you become?

If you hang out with sardines, according to the law of averages, you'll be a sardine too. If you want to be a shark, you need to surround yourself with sharks.

SURROUND YOURSELF WITH CHAMPIONS

Make a list of all the good qualities in your favorite people. These are some of the qualities that can help you become a champion.

DRAW THE TREE OF YOUR LIFE!

Then list all the things in your environment that will feed your roots and help you grow strong—just like the redwood.

WHAT HAVE WE LEARNED?

CHAMPION'S ENVIRONMENT

Be aware of the environment you're in and create a Champion's environment for yourself.

Your environment can be changed. What do you want to be, a bonsai or a redwood?

WILLPOWER

Your environment is stronger than your willpower.

Team power—1 + 1 is greater than 2.

COPY SUCCESS

Learn from the best and copy success—it can shorten your path to success!

Make decisions quickly and change your mind slowly.

SWIM LIKE A SHARK

The law of averages—it's impossible to swim like a shark if you hang out with sardines.

Code 10

Champion's Questions

TAKE POSITIVE ACTION TO GET THE RESULTS YOU WANT!

The first CHAMPION'S Question: "Does it ADVANCE ME?"

We met this question in Code 2. We will briefly remind you of it here since it's very important!

All our results in life come from: Thoughts—Emotions—Actions—Results. With the help of this question, you create a space to stop between emotions and actions. This pause, even for a second or two, and the question "Does it advance me?" will help you avoid taking actions that aren't helpful, and **prevent you from getting unwanted results in your life**!

Asking "Does it advance me?" gives you **a sneak peek into your future**! We don't have the ability to operate a time machine, but that pause and question can help you see the result you would get in the future following your action. This way you can choose whether to act or not.

In Code 2 we discussed the Champion's Question in a limited aspect. Now we want to teach you **a significant extension of this question**. It has two parts:

THE FIRST PART, as you've already learned, addresses your choice to act. Does it advance me?

THE SECOND PART, will this choice bring happiness to **me and everyone around me**?

THE QUESTION EXAMINES WHETHER THE ACTION ADVANCES YOU OR THOSE AROUND YOU: your family, friends, teachers, etc., and whether it brings happiness to you as well as those around you. Will you and those around you be happy following your actions?

You can't choose the situations or events that'll happen to you in life. You're not responsible or in control of the things that other people do, but you can choose how you handle a situation.

For example, if a kid in your class uses bad language and calls your mom a name, that doesn't make what that person says a reality. The reality is how you choose to react to the incident. Why should you even respond to that person's statements? The reality you wish to create for yourself will be the one to determine your future!

You're the director of your life; you're writing the script and you won't let anyone hold the pen and write the script for you!

In the 2006 World Cup soccer final, two teams reached the final—the French team and the Italian team. The star and captain of the French national team was **the player Zinedine Zidane.** He was one of the best and most famous players in the world. The game ended in a draw and then there was extra time. During the extra time, an Italian player approached the French player and called his sister names. The French player got upset and headbutted the Italian player. The referee issued a red card to the French player, which meant he was sent off the field and his team was left with one less player and lost to the Italian team. The French player came off the field in disgrace, his entire career ruined in that moment on the field. Why did he decide to react so aggressively? Did this action advance him? Did this action help his sister, or the fans watching?

The reality was that the Italian player cursed his sister, but so what? **Zidane's reaction determined his reality.** He could have chosen a more advancing response, for himself, for his sister, for his team and for all the team's fans.

Another STEP FORWARD

As we explained in Code 2, our ultimate target is to help you control your **thoughts**. The extended question toward those around you also applies to the choice of **thoughts** and not only to the choice of actions.

That means, the extended question of "Does it advance me and those around me?", will help you choose more useful thoughts from the first moment. It'll also guide you toward what makes you and those around you happy, and the understanding of action by conscious choice.

Conscious choice is a choice that relates to both parts: does it help both you and those around you? Does it bring you and them satisfaction and happiness?

You can't choose the event, but you can choose how you react to it.

"WHAT will DETERMINE our reality isn't what's HAPPENING, BUT RATHER our REACTION to what's happening!"

(Dr. Michal Solomonovich)

The SECOND CHAMPION'S Question: "How Can I?"

CHAMPIONS ALWAYS ASK "HOW CAN I?". OTHERS DEAL WITH "WHY NOT?" "WHY NOT ME?" "WHY NOT NOW?".

Most people ask, "Why not?" but champions ask "How Can I?" because they're always looking for ways to overcome and achieve their goals.

The Champion's Question "How Can I?" shows you there is always a way, you just need to find it. And it can be used for internal and external aspects.

ON THE EXTERNAL ASPECT: How can I help someone?

ON THE INTERNAL ASPECT: Despite your inner thoughts, you'll still think "How can I do it?"

In thinking "How can I?", you see there are always solutions, you just need to find them. You need to set ambitions and goals, then you figure out how to achieve them.

ALWAYS THINK: HOW CAN I?

We'll illustrate this idea with a simple example: A car is driving through the dark with its headlights on and only a small section of the road ahead is lit. The driver still continues because they know the road exists further ahead even if they are currently unable to see it. The question "How can I?" allows the driver to advance toward their goal, one small step at a time. The main thing is to keep moving forward.

The THIRD CHAMPION'S Question: "What's great about it?"

As part of the conscious choice we spoke about earlier, we'll show you how to adopt a positive approach to life. Think about everything that's happening to you and ask yourself, **"What's great about it?".**

In every situation in life, even in difficult times when there's failure, fear, illness, death, accidents, loss and so on, there is always a lesson you can learn. You must ask yourself: What can I learn from the situation? What is the opportunity here? You can look at difficult situations as closed doors, but there will always be a new door that opens for you.

The law of polarity says that every state has its opposite state. Every difficulty has an opportunity. Every failure has a great lesson in life. In every evil there is good.

GOOD AND BAD ARE RELATIVE AND NOT ABSOLUTE CONCEPTS.

We're not here to say that a difficult event is a great event. But the difference between champions and others is that champions know how to ask, even in difficult moments, what they can learn from this.

The word "great" is a positive word and so opposed to a negative event that when it's used in the context of a negative event it requires you to think differently.

After difficult events in life, you'll see that there's also room to learn and grow. For example, if you got a low grade on an important test but ask yourself, "What's great about it?", it'll allow you to see what is still great about this situation. The low grade is great because it allows you to learn from your mistakes, understand that you need to invest more and work harder for the next test.

Maybe you wanted to make the school football team or, get the lead part in the school play and you didn't make it. Asking "What's great about it?" will allow you to learn from your mistakes and change something about what you're doing. Maybe that means more practice or asking for advice—whatever it is that'll get you where you need to be for next time.

The FOURTH CHAMPION'S Question: "How would the PERSON I want to be BEHAVE in this SITUATION?"

If you want to be an excellent student or a talented basketball player, long before you reach your goal, you have to think and act **today** like the person you want to be in the future.

You can't expect to get there without putting in the effort.

The Law of Sacrifice states that you must be willing to give to receive. There's no reward and results without investing effort.

You're amazing and you have the potential to reach your "Greatest You" but it won't happen by itself.

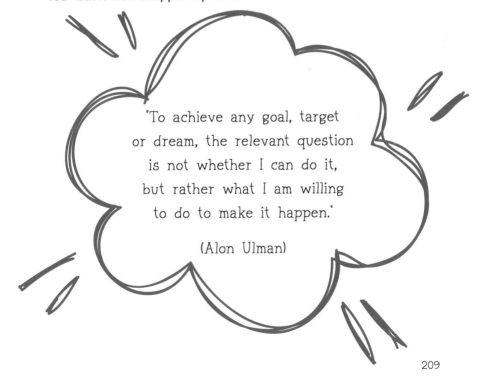

"To achieve any goal, target or dream, the relevant question is not whether I can do it, but rather what I am willing to do to make it happen."

(Alon Ulman)

This book focuses on practical success, so the question you need to ask yourself in order to get the results is this:

WHAT ARE YOU WILLING TO DO TO MAKE THAT HAPPEN?

What price are you willing to pay? Not in dollars, but in effort. How much are you willing to put in, here and now, to reach your goals?

Most people don't want to make the effort now. You could promise yourself that if you get to where you want to be, then you'll start making the effort—but the world doesn't work that way. The Law of Sacrifice always works.

FIRST EFFORT AND THEN RESULTS, IN EVERY AREA OF LIFE

If you want to be a champion athlete, you need to act like a champion athlete today. If you're persistent and make progress, you can become that athlete. Today you need to train, sleep well, eat healthy food, so that you can work toward positive results.

THINK AND ACT LIKE THE PERSON YOU WANT TO BE

If you want to be an excellent student, you need to think and act like an excellent student today. If you're persistent and make progress, you'll get to be that student. **As of today** you need to do your homework, you need to be organized, you need to listen in class. This is how you move toward the results you want.

The question, "How would the person I want to be behave in this situation?" will help you reach your Champion's Vision faster.

You should **think and act today as if you've already reached your goal**.

If you want to be a champion basketball player, then today you need to start thinking and acting like that player!

If you want to be an excellent student, then today you need to start thinking and acting like that student!

Champions engage in actions that make them progress. They perform daily actions that help them toward achieving their Champion's Vision.

There's no point in waiting for the future, the best time to start is now, without excuses and delaying until tomorrow, or next week. Start today, even if it's by taking small steps, to think and act like the person you want to be.

IF YOU WANT CHANGE, BE THE CHANGE!

You're the director of your life! If you want change, you have to make it yourself, no one else can do it for you.

The FIFTH CHAMPION'S Question:
"Is my EFFORT aimed toward SUCCESS?"

An effective and important Champion's Question is, "Is my effort aimed toward success?". Effort aimed and directed toward success is even more important than talent for success in life. There are three sub-questions for this:

○ The first, "What are the rules?".

○ The second, "What do I consider a win?".

○ And the third, "How close am I to my goal?".

For example, in a basketball game, a player who comes on the court aims toward success. They know what the rules are; they know what's considered a win (their team scoring the highest number of points); during the game they can see how they're doing and how much time is left in the game.

This applies to other fields of your life. We want you to know the rules of the game, what you consider to be a win and where you stand at each stage toward reaching your goal.

WHAT WOULD THE PERSON YOU WANT TO BE DO?

Imagine and write a TV interview where the person you are today is interviewing you in the future about your success. Have you achieved all your goals? Talk about how you did it.

EVERYTHING'S A LESSON: WHAT'S GREAT ABOUT IT?

Write or draw an event in your life where you didn't get what you want.

Ask yourself: "What's great about it?" and write how this eventually helped you. What was the lesson you learned?

WHAT HAVE WE LEARNED?

"DOES IT ADVANCE ME?"

"Does it advance me?" the extended question.

You can't choose the event, but you can choose how to react to it.

"HOW CAN I?"

Champions are always looking at "How Can I?" rather than "Why not?".

What's great about it? Look for lessons, even in bad situations.

How would the person you want to be behave in this situation?

WHAT YOU'RE WILLING TO DO

To achieve any goal, target or dream, the relevant question is not whether you can do it, but rather what you're willing to do to make it happen.

BE THE CHANGE!

If you want change, be the change!

Is your effort aimed toward success? This is even more important than talent for success in life.

A Note to Parents

We believe that parents are leaders. You have the power to guide your child to practical success in life. This book is a helping hand, giving them the five components of growth—knowledge, tools, method, mentoring and environment. These components will be essential for the journey from their 'You of Today' toward their 'Greatest You' in all areas of life, including school, family, friends, sports, hobbies and so on. The things written in this book are taken from the world of leadership and are simple and easy to implement.

The first thing to note in this journey is that there are always going to be challenges within parenting and growing up and this book is about progress, not perfection. The methods here are adapted from an educational e-learning program in Israel called the Winner's Code Junior and it has helped thousands of children. The success of the program is proven by an evaluation study made by the Henrietta Sold Insitute, the Isralei national institute for research in behavioural sciences. The program is approved in the database of educational programs at the Isralei Ministry of Education. We focus on being consistent, having goals, building confidence with positive language and feedback, instead of criticism—to enable kids to deal with obstacles more effectively, so they can develop problem-solving skills they will use as building blocks for their future. It's important for children to see that challenges can be overcome and that they are an opportunity to grow. We know that every child is talented, but even more important than talent, is the ability to pick yourself up and move forward. What do successful people have in common? The first quality is resilience. The ability to cope, move on and overcome.

The best thing you can do as a parent is talk to your child—and not just about their own goals from using this book. Talk about your aspirations too, so you can share and mark your achievements and goals as a family. You can do this together before the beginning of the school year, on a family day, or at any other time that feels right for you. Your family is your team and it's important that each family member knows and feels this, no one has your back more than family, right? We hope this book is a tool for growth and that it can open up a positive discussion in your family about goals and the steps you can take to achieve them.

Appendix

GRADUATION CERTIFICATE

This is to certify that

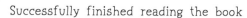

....

Successfully finished reading the book

CHAMPION!

EVERYTHING YOU NEED TO BE YOUR GREATEST YOU

- Starting today I make the decision to be a champion in my life!

- I'm the director of my life and write the script in it!

- I write a Champion's Vision for myself, setting goals and targets and will work to achieve them.

- Before each action I'll ask myself the Champion's Question Does this advance me?

- I act according to the super-principle anything you want to get, give!

- I don't give up because otherwise I'll never know how close I was to success.

- I always remember to achieve any goal, target or dream, the relevant question isn't whether I can do it, but rather what am I willing to do to make it happen?

THE BIG THREE ON THE WAY TO MY CHAMPION'S VISION

1ST GOAL — SCHOOL

Why is this goal important to me?

How will I feel when I achieve this goal?

How will this goal advance me in life?

2ND GOAL — PERSONAL

Why is this goal important to me?

How will I feel when I achieve this goal?

How will this goal advance me in life?

3RD GOAL — SOCIAL

Why is this goal important to me?

How will I feel when I achieve this goal?

How will this goal advance me in life?

THE MONTHLY LIGHTHOUSE

1ST TARGET — SCHOOL

Actions I'll take to get there

Who?...

What?..

When?...

2ND TARGET — PERSONAL

Actions I'll take to get there

Who?...

What?..

When?...

3RD TARGET — SOCIAL

Actions I'll take to get there

Who?...

What?..

When?...

WHAT DID I ACHIEVE THIS MONTH?

1ST TARGET — SCHOOL

What results did I get?

What were the actions that led me to it?

2ND TARGET — PERSONAL

What results did I get?

What were the actions that led me to it?

3RD TARGET — SOCIAL

What results did I get?

What were the actions that led me to it?

What can I learn from this for next time?

....
....
....
....

What opportunities did this open up for me?

....
....
....
....

Who should I be grateful for this month?

....
....
....
....